D1144542

Mary C. Schlembach
William H. Mischo
Editors

Electronic Resources
and Services
in Sci-Tech Libraries

Electronic Resources and Services in Sci-Tech Libraries
has been co-published simultaneously as *Science &*
Technology Libraries, Volume 20, Numbers 2/3 2001.

Pre-publication
REVIEWS,
COMMENTARIES,
EVALUATIONS . . .

"THOUGHT-PROVOKING. . . .
Presents issues and solutions
that librarians can analyze and then
modify to apply within their own institutions. I especially enjoyed Kristi
Jensen's chapter, a well-crafted
study that demonstrates that the
electronic dissemination of government documents is creating a large
body of literature that is not trace-
able by traditional research library
tools."

Kate Thomes, MA
Head
Bevier Engineering Library
University of Pittsburgh

The Haworth Information Press
An Imprint of The Haworth Press, Inc.

Electronic Resources
and Services
in Sci-Tech Libraries

Electronic Resources and Services in Sci-Tech Libraries has been co-published simultaneously as *Science & Technology Libraries*, Volume 20, Numbers 2/3 2001.

The *Science & Technology Libraries* Monographic "Separates"

Below is a list of "separates," which in serials librarianship means a special issue simultaneously published as a special journal issue or double-issue *and* as a "separate" hardbound monograph. (This is a format which we also call a "DocuSerial.")

"Separates" are published because specialized libraries or professionals may wish to purchase a specific thematic issue by itself in a format which can be separately cataloged and shelved, as opposed to purchasing the journal on an on-going basis. Faculty members may also more easily consider a "separate" for classroom adoption.

"Separates" are carefully classified separately with the major book jobbers so that the journal tie-in can be noted on new book order slips to avoid duplicate purchasing.

You may wish to visit Haworth's website at . . .

http://www.HaworthPress.com

. . . to search our online catalog for complete tables of contents of these separates and related publications.

You may also call 1-800-HAWORTH (outside US/Canada: 607-722-5857), or Fax: 1-800-895-0582 (outside US/Canada: 607-771-0012), or e-mail at:

getinfo@haworthpressinc.com

Electronic Resources and Services in Sci-Tech Libraries, edited by Mary C. Schlembach, BS, MLS, and William H. Mischo, BA, MA (Vol. 20, No. 2/3, 2001). *Examines collection development, reference service, and information service in science and technology libraries.*

Engineering Libraries: Building Collections and Delivering Services, edited by Thomas W. Conkling, BS, MLS, and Linda R. Musser, BS, MS (Vol. 19, No. 3/4, 2001). *"Highly useful. The range of topics is broad, from collections to user services . . . most of the authors provide extra value by focusing on points of special interest. Of value to almost all librarians or information specialists in academic or special libraries, or as a supplementary text for graduate library courses." (Susan Davis Herring, MLS, PhD, Engineering Reference Librarian, M. Louis Salmon Library, University of Alabama, Huntsville)*

Electronic Expectations: Science Journals on the Web, by Tony Stankus, MLS (Vol. 18, No. 2/3, 1999). *Separates the hype about electronic journals from the realities that they will bring. This book provides a complete tutorial review of the literature that relates to the rise of electronic journals in the sciences and explores the many cost factors that may prevent electronic journals from becoming revolutionary in the research industry.*

Digital Libraries: Philosophies, Technical Design Considerations, and Example Scenarios, edited by David Stern (Vol. 17, No. 3/4, 1999). *"Digital Libraries: Philosophies, Technical Design Considerations, and Example Scenarios targets the general librarian population and does a good job of opening eyes to the impact that digital library projects are already having in our automated libraries." (Kimberly J. Parker, MILS, Electronic Publishing & Collections Librarian, Yale University Library)*

Sci/Tech Librarianship: Education and Training, edited by Julie Hallmark, PhD, and Ruth K. Seidman, MSLS (Vol. 17, No. 2, 1998). *"Insightful, informative, and right-on-the-mark. . . . This collection provides a much-needed view of the education of sci/tech librarians." (Michael R. Leach, AB, Director, Physics Research Library, Harvard University)*

Chemical Librarianship: Challenges and Opportunities, edited by Arleen N. Somerville (Vol. 16, No. 3/4, 1997). *"Presents a most satisfying collection of articles that will be of interest, first and foremost, to chemistry librarians, but also to science librarians working in other science disciplines within academic settings." (Barbara List, Director, Science and Engineering Libraries, Columbia University, New York, New York)*

History of Science and Technology: A Sampler of Centers and Collections of Distinction, edited by Cynthia Steinke, MS (Vol. 14, No. 4, 1995). *"A 'grand tour' of history of science and technology collections that is of great interest to scholars, students and librarians." (Jay K. Lucker, AB, MSLS, Director of Libraries, Massachusetts Institute of Technology; Lecturer in Science and Technology, Simmons College, Graduate School of Library and Information Science)*

Instruction for Information Access in Sci-Tech Libraries, edited by Cynthia Steinke, MS (Vol. 14, No. 2, 1994). *"A refreshing mix of user education programs and contain[s] many examples of good practice." (Library Review and Reference Reviews)*

Scientific and Clinical Literature for the Decade of the Brain, edited by Tony Stankus, MLS (Vol. 13, No. 3/4, 1993). *"This format combined with selected book and journal title lists is very convenient for life science, social science, or general reference librarians/bibliographers who wish to review the area or get up to speed quickly." (Ruth Lewis, MLS, Biology Librarian, Washington University, St. Louis, Missouri)*

Sci-Tech Libraries of the Future, edited by Cynthia Steinke, MS (Vol. 12, No. 4 and Vol. 13, No. 1, 1993). *"Very timely. . . . Will be of interest to all libraries confronted with changes in technology, information formats, and user expectations." (LA Record)*

Science Librarianship at America's Liberal Arts Colleges: Working Librarians Tell Their Stories, edited by Tony Stankus, MLS (Vol. 12, No. 3, 1992). *"For those teetering on the tightrope between the needs and desires of science faculty and liberal arts librarianship, this book brings a sense of balance." (Teresa R. Faust, MLS, Science Reference Librarian, Wake Forest University)*

Biographies of Scientists for Sci-Tech Libraries: Adding Faces to the Facts, edited by Tony Stankus, MLS (Vol. 11, No. 4, 1992). *"A guide to biographies of scientists from a wide variety of scientific fields, identifying titles that reveal the personality of the biographee as well as contributions to his/her field." (Sci Tech Book News)*

Information Seeking and Communicating Behavior of Scientists and Engineers, edited by Cynthia Steinke, MS (Vol. 11, No. 3, 1991). *"Unequivocally recommended. . . . The subject is one of importance to most university libraries, which are actively engaged in addressing user needs as a framework for library services." (New Library World)*

Technology Transfer: The Role of the Sci-Tech Librarian, edited by Cynthia Steinke, MS (Vol. 11, No. 2, 1991). *"Educates the reader about the role of information professionals in the multifaceted technology transfer process." (Journal of Chemical Information and Computer Sciences)*

Electronic Information Systems in Sci-Tech Libraries, edited by Cynthia Steinke, MS (Vol. 11, No. 1, 1990). *"Serves to illustrate the possibilities for effective networking from any library/information facility to any other geographical point." (Library Journal)*

The Role of Trade Literature in Sci-Tech Libraries, edited by Ellis Mount, DLS (Vol. 10, No. 4, 1990). *"A highly useful resource to identify and discuss the subject of manufacturers' catalogs and their historical as well as practical value to the profession of librarianship. Dr. Mount has made an outstanding contribution." (Academic Library Book Review)*

Role of Standards in Sci-Tech Libraries, edited by Ellis Mount, DLS (Vol. 10, No. 3, 1990). *Required reading for any librarian who has been asked to identify standards and specifications.*

Relation of Sci-Tech Information to Environmental Studies, edited by Ellis Mount, DLS (Vol. 10, No. 2, 1990). *"A timely and important book that illustrates the nature and use of sci-tech information in relation to the environment." (The Bulletin of Science, Technology & Society)*

End-User Training for Sci-Tech Databases, edited by Ellis Mount, DLS (Vol. 10, No. 1, 1990). *"This is a timely publication for those of us involved in conducting online searches in special libraries where our users have a detailed knowledge of their subject areas." (Australian Library Review)*

Sci-Tech Archives and Manuscript Collections, edited by Ellis Mount, DLS (Vol. 9, No. 4, 1989). *Gain valuable information on the ways in which sci-tech archival material is being handled and preserved in various institutions and organizations.*

Collection Management in Sci-Tech Libraries, edited by Ellis Mount, DLS (Vol. 9, No. 3, 1989). *"An interesting and timely survey of current issues in collection management as they pertain to science and technology libraries." (Barbara A. List, AMLS, Coordinator of Collection Development, Science & Technology Research Center, and Editor, New Technical Books, The Research Libraries, New York Public Library)*

The Role of Conference Literature in Sci-Tech Libraries, edited by Ellis Mount, DLS (Vol. 9, No. 2, 1989). *"The volume constitutes a valuable overview of the issues posed for librarians and users by one of the most frustrating and yet important sources of scientific and technical information." (Australian Library Review)*

Adaptation of Turnkey Computer Systems in Sci-Tech Libraries, edited by Ellis Mount, DLS (Vol. 9, No. 1, 1989). *"Interesting and useful. . . . The book addresses the problems and benefits associated with the installation of a turnkey or ready-made computer system in a scientific or technical library." (Information Retrieval & Library Automation)*

Sci-Tech Libraries Serving Zoological Gardens, edited by Ellis Mount, DLS (Vol. 8, No. 4, 1989). *"Reviews the history and development of six major zoological garden libraries in the U.S." (Australian Library Review)*

Libraries Serving Science-Oriented and Vocational High Schools, edited by Ellis Mount, DLS (Vol. 8, No. 3, 1989). *A wealth of information on the special collections of science-oriented and vocational high schools, with a look at their services, students, activities, and problems.*

Sci-Tech Library Networks Within Organizations, edited by Ellis Mount, DLS (Vol. 8, No. 2, 1988). *Offers thorough descriptions of sci-tech library networks in which their members have a common sponsorship or ownership.*

One Hundred Years of Sci-Tech Libraries: A Brief History, edited by Ellis Mount, DLS (Vol. 8, No. 1, 1988). *"Should be read by all those considering, or who are already involved in, information retrieval, whether in Sci-tech libraries or others." (Library Resources & Technical Services)*

Alternative Careers in Sci-Tech Information Service, edited by Ellis Mount, DLS (Vol. 7, No. 4, 1987). *Here is an eye-opening look at alternative careers for professionals with a sci-tech background, including librarians, scientists, and engineers.*

Preservation and Conservation of Sci-Tech Materials, edited by Ellis Mount, DLS (Vol. 7, No. 3, 1987). *"This cleverly coordinated work is essential reading for library school students and practicing librarians. . . . Recommended reading." (Science Books and Films)*

Sci-Tech Libraries Serving Societies and Institutions, edited by Ellis Mount, DLS (Vol. 7, No. 2, 1987). *"Of most interest to special librarians, providing them with some insight into sci-tech libraries and their activities as well as a means of identifying specialized services and collections which may be of use to them." (Sci-Tech Libraries)*

Innovations in Planning Facilities for Sci-Tech Libraries, edited by Ellis Mount, DLS (Vol. 7, No. 1, 1986). *"Will prove invaluable to any librarian establishing a new library or contemplating expansion." (Australasian College Libraries)*

Role of Computers in Sci-Tech Libraries, edited by Ellis Mount, DLS (Vol. 6, No. 4, 1986). *"A very readable text. . . . I am including a number of the articles in the student reading list." (C. Bull, Kingstec Community College, Kentville, Nova Scotia, Canada)*

Weeding of Collections in Sci-Tech Libraries, edited by Ellis Mount, DLS (Vol. 6, No. 3, 1986). *"A useful publication. . . . Should be in every science and technology library." (Rivernia Library Review)*

Sci-Tech Libraries in Museums and Aquariums, edited by Ellis Mount, DLS (Vol. 6, No. 1/2, 1985). *"Useful to libraries in museums and aquariums for its descriptive and practical information." (The Association for Information Management)*

Data Manipulation in Sci-Tech Libraries, edited by Ellis Mount, DLS (Vol. 5, No. 4, 1985). *"Papers in this volume present evidence of the growing sophistication in the manipulation of data by information personnel." (Sci-Tech Book News)*

Role of Maps in Sci-Tech Libraries, edited by Ellis Mount, DLS (Vol. 5, No. 3, 1985). *Learn all about the acquisition of maps and the special problems of their storage and preservation in this insightful book.*

Fee-Based Services in Sci-Tech Libraries, edited by Ellis Mount, DLS (Vol. 5, No. 2, 1985). *"Highly recommended. Any librarian will find something of interest in this volume." (Australasian College Libraries)*

Serving End-Users in Sci-Tech Libraries, edited by Ellis Mount, DLS (Vol. 5, No. 1, 1984). *"Welcome and indeed interesting reading. . . . a useful acquisition for anyone starting out in one or more of the areas covered." (Australasian College Libraries)*

Management of Sci-Tech Libraries, edited by Ellis Mount, DLS (Vol. 4, No. 3/4, 1984). *Become better equipped to tackle difficult staffing, budgeting, and personnel challenges with this essential volume on managing different types of sci-tech libraries.*

Collection Development in Sci-Tech Libraries, edited by Ellis Mount, DLS (Vol. 4, No. 2, 1984). *"Well-written by authors who work in the field they are discussing. Should be of value to librarians whose collections cover a wide range of scientific and technical fields." (Library Acquisitions: Practice and Theory)*

Role of Serials in Sci-Tech Libraries, edited by Ellis Mount, DLS (Vol. 4, No. 1, 1983). *"Some interesting nuggets to offer dedicated serials librarians and users of scientific journal literature. . . . Outlines the direction of some major changes already occurring in scientific journal publishing and serials management." (Serials Review)*

Planning Facilities for Sci-Tech Libraries, edited by Ellis Mount, DLS (Vol. 3, No. 4, 1983). *"Will be of interest to special librarians who are contemplating the building of new facilities or the renovating and adaptation of existing facilities in the near future. . . . A useful manual based on actual experiences." (Sci-Tech News)*

Monographs in Sci-Tech Libraries, edited by Ellis Mount, DLS (Vol. 3, No. 3, 1983). *This insightful book addresses the present contributions monographs are making in sci-tech libraries as well as their probable role in the future.*

Role of Translations in Sci-Tech Libraries, edited by Ellis Mount, DLS (Vol. 3, No. 2, 1983). *"Good required reading in a course on special libraries in library school. It would also be useful to any librarian who handles the ordering of translations." (Sci-Tech News)*

Online versus Manual Searching in Sci-Tech Libraries, edited by Ellis Mount, DLS (Vol. 3, No. 1, 1982). *An authoritative volume that examines the role that manual searches play in academic, public, corporate, and hospital libraries.*

Document Delivery for Sci-Tech Libraries, edited by Ellis Mount, DLS (Vol. 2, No. 4, 1982). *Touches on important aspects of document delivery and the place each aspect holds in the overall scheme of things.*

Cataloging and Indexing for Sci-Tech Libraries, edited by Ellis Mount, DLS (Vol. 2, No. 3, 1982). *Diverse and authoritative views on the problems of cataloging and indexing in sci-tech libraries.*

Role of Patents in Sci-Tech Libraries, edited by Ellis Mount, DLS (Vol. 2, No. 2, 1982). *A fascinating look at the nature of patents and the complicated, ever-changing set of indexes and computerized databases devoted to facilitating the identification and retrieval of patents.*

Current Awareness Services in Sci-Tech Libraries, edited by Ellis Mount, DLS (Vol. 2, No. 1, 1982). *An interesting and comprehensive look at the many forms of current awareness services that sci-tech libraries offer.*

Role of Technical Reports in Sci-Tech Libraries, edited by Ellis Mount, DLS (Vol. 1, No. 4, 1982). *Recommended reading not only for science and technology librarians, this unique volume is specifically devoted to the analysis of problems, innovative practices, and advances relating to the control and servicing of technical reports.*

Training of Sci-Tech Librarians and Library Users, edited by Ellis Mount, DLS (Vol. 1, No. 3, 1981). *Here is a crucial overview of the current and future issues in the training of science and engineering librarians as well as instruction for users of these libraries.*

Networking in Sci-Tech Libraries and Information Centers, edited by Ellis Mount, DLS (Vol. 1, No. 2, 1981). *Here is an entire volume devoted to the topic of cooperative projects and library networks among sci-tech libraries.*

Planning for Online Search Service in Sci-Tech Libraries, edited by Ellis Mount, DLS (Vol. 1, No. 1, 1981). *Covers the most important issue to consider when planning for online search services.*

Electronic Resources
and Services
in Sci-Tech Libraries

Mary C. Schlembach
William H. Mischo
Editors

Electronic Resources and Services in Sci-Tech Libraries has been co-published simultaneously as *Science & Technology Libraries*, Volume 20, Numbers 2/3 2001.

The Haworth Information Press
An Imprint of
The Haworth Press, Inc.
New York • London • Oxford

Published by

The Haworth Information Press®,10 Alice Street, Binghamton, NY 13904-1580 USA

The Haworth Information Press® is an imprint of The Haworth Press, Inc., 10 Alice Street, Binghamtom, NY 13904-1580 USA.

Electronic Resources and Services in Sci-Tech Libraries has been co-published simultaneously as *Science & Technology Libraries*™, Volume 20, Numbers 2/3 2001.

The development, preparation, and publication of this work has been undertaken with great care. However, the publisher, employees, editors, and agents of The Haworth Press and all imprints of The Haworth Press, Inc., including The Haworth Medical Press® and Pharmaceutical Products Press®, are not responsible for any errors contained herein or for consequences that may ensue from use of materials or information contained in this work. Opinions expressed by the author(s) are not necessarily those of The Haworth Press, Inc. With regard to case studies, identities and circumstances of individuals discussed herein have been changed to protect confidentiality. Any resemblance to actual persons, living or dead, is entirely coincidental.

Cover design by Thomas J. Mayshock Jr.

Library of Congress Cataloging-in-Publication Data

Electronic resources and services in sci-tech libraries / Mary C. Schlembach, William H. Mischo, editors.
        p. cm.
    Includes bibliographical references and index.
    ISBN 0-7890-1934-5 (alk. paper) – ISBN 0-7890-1935-3 (pbk : alk. paper)
    1. Technical libraries. 2. Scientific libraries. 3. Technology–Electronic information resources. 4. Science–Electronic information resources. 5. Online information services. 6. Libraries and electronic publishing. I. Schlembach, Mary C. II. Mischo, William H. III. Science & technology libraries.
Z675.T3 E435 2002
026.6–dc21   2002003159

Indexing, Abstracting & Website/Internet Coverage

This section provides you with a list of major indexing & abstracting services. That is to say, each service began covering this periodical during the year noted in the right column. Most Websites which are listed below have indicated that they will either post, disseminate, compile, archive, cite or alert their own Website users with research-based content from this work. (This list is as current as the copyright date of this publication.)

(continued)

(continued)

*Special Bibliographic Notes related to special journal issues
(separates) and indexing/abstracting:*

- indexing/abstracting services in this list will also cover material in any "separate" that is co-published simultaneously with Haworth's special thematic journal issue or DocuSerial. Indexing/abstracting usually covers material at the article/chapter level.
- monographic co-editions are intended for either non-subscribers or libraries which intend to purchase a second copy for their circulating collections.
- monographic co-editions are reported to all jobbers/wholesalers/approval plans. The source journal is listed as the "series" to assist the prevention of duplicate purchasing in the same manner utilized for books-in-series.
- to facilitate user/access services all indexing/abstracting services are encouraged to utilize the co-indexing entry note indicated at the bottom of the first page of each article/chapter/contribution.
- this is intended to assist a library user of any reference tool (whether print, electronic, online, or CD-ROM) to locate the monographic version if the library has purchased this version but not a subscription to the source journal.
- individual articles/chapters in any Haworth publication are also available through the Haworth Document Delivery Service (HDDS).

Electronic Resources and Services in Sci-Tech Libraries

CONTENTS

ELECTRONIC SERVICES

ABOUT THE EDITORS

Mary C. Schlembach, BS, MLS, is Assistant Engineering Librarian for Digital Projects at the University of Illinois at Urbana-Champaign. She was the editor of the American Society for Engineering Education's Engineering Libraries Division publication *Union List of Technical Reports, Standards, and Patents in Engineering Libraries,* Fourth Edition.

William H. Mischo, BA, MA, is Head, Grainger Engineering Library Information Center, and Professor of Library Administration at the University of Illinois at Urbana-Champaign. Before joining the UIUC Library in 1982, he was at OCLC, Inc., and Iowa State University. He has published over 45 articles in library and information science journals and conference proceedings, and has presented at conferences of the American Library Association, the Special Libraries Association, the American Society for Information Science and Technology, and the American Society for Engineering Education. He presented the keynote address at The XML Workshop for Electronic Journals (2001) in Tokyo, Japan.

Introduction

Advanced technology is indistinguishable from magic.

–Arthur C. Clarke

This special, thematic volume focuses on Electronic Resources and Services. Clearly, electronic technologies have produced revolutionary changes in the daily activities of science librarians. However, the fundamental role of librarians remains the same: to collect source materials, organize those materials, and provide effective and efficient access to those materials. Electronic technologies provide librarians with new mechanisms and tools to accomplish these traditional functions in a distributed and virtual environment. Electronic resources and services emphasize the library as function, in addition to place. The articles in this volume have been selected to represent various facets of these new technologies. The articles can generally be divided between the areas of electronic services and resources. Several of the papers discuss the relationship between these two areas.

The volume begins with an overview of electronic resources at the University of Arizona. Paul J. Bracke, in "Access to Remote Electronic Resources at the University of Arizona," discusses methods to control and manage electronic access through the use of proxy servers and Persistent Uniform Resource Locators (PURLs).

Following are two papers describing the strengths and weaknesses of information retrieval technologies related to specific subject areas of sci/tech libraries. "Providing Access to Online Government Documents in an Academic Research Collection: A Case Study in the Geosciences,"

[Haworth co-indexing entry note]: "Introduction." Schlembach, Mary C. Co-published simultaneously in *Science & Technology Libraries* (The Haworth Information Press, an imprint of The Haworth Press, Inc.) Vol. 20, No. 2/3, 2001, pp. 1-3; and: *Electronic Resources and Services in Sci-Tech Libraries* (ed: Mary C. Schlembach, and William H. Mischo) The Haworth Information Press, an imprint of The Haworth Press, Inc., 2001, pp. 1-3. Single or multiple copies of this article are available for a fee from The Haworth Document Delivery Service [1-800-HAWORTH, 9:00 a.m. - 5:00 p.m. (EST). E-mail address: getinfo@haworthpress inc.com].

1

by Kristi Jensen, describes the difficulties of finding geotechnical information on the Web and the relationship between traditional indexing and abstracting services and Web resources. As more individuals and organizations begin to self-publish electronic documents, there will be a new set of strategies needed for search and discovery for these documents. Addressing the problems of displaying fonts, symbols, arrangements, and alignments, Tim Cole outlines the strategies for "Publishing Mathematics on the Web." Properly rendering mathematical equations in a Web environment continues to be a difficult, yet dynamic aspect of the sci/tech literature.

Electronic journals have become a primary element of library collections of all types and sizes. Winnie S. Chan discusses the benefits of using an e-resource registry in combination with Web-based services to provide enhanced access in "Creative Applications of a Web-Based E-Resource Registry." This article describes methods to extend access to e-resources and integrate e-journal functionality with other Web-based local applications. It is always important to evaluate library services and electronic journals are no exception. "Performance Measures for Electronic Journals: A User-Centered Approach" by Julie Hurd, Deborah Blecic, and Ann Robinson describe a user-centered evaluation of electronic journals. Some very useful models of research methodologies and performance measures are included in the article.

The last article of the electronic resources portion focuses on preprint services. As journal prices increase dramatically and dissatisfaction with the publisher-centric scholarly communication model grows, scientists, librarians, and university administrators are examining alternatives to traditional publication models. "A Brief History of E-Prints and the Opportunities They Open for Science Librarians" by Kenneth L. Carriveau outlines the history of preprint servers and speculates on what the future may hold for this important technology.

Electronic services continue to expand on many of the sci/tech libraries traditional user-centered functions. For example, many libraries have begun to offer remote electronic reference or are planning to implement e-reference soon. Deborah L. Helman describes the e-reference services implemented at the Massachusetts Institute of Technology in "Bringing the Human Touch to Digital Library Services." This paper discusses the major issues and technologies involved in bringing electronic reference services out to the user and points out several often overlooked factors.

As electronic services expand and improve, the need for information literacy skills that allow users to effectively interact with new products and technologies becomes important. Marianne Stowell Bracke and Lori Jean Critz present a broad overview of new information literacy technology in "Re-Envisioning Instruction for the Electronic Environment of a 21st Century Science-Engineering Library."

Other traditional academic library services have also benefited from being transformed into electronic-based services. Tina Chrzastowski describes the implementation of an electronic reserves system in "Electronic Reserves in the Science Library: Tips, Techniques, and User Perceptions." The article also suggests methodologies for on-going user studies to improve current e-reserves systems.

One of the important aspects of these electronic technologies is the ability to 'push' services out to the remote users. This is a feature of electronic full-text journals, online A & I services, and current awareness services. Mary Schlembach's article "Trends in Current Awareness Services" explores new ways of providing electronic current awareness services covering both journals and books to researchers. Finally, William Mischo, in "Library Portals, Simultaneous Search, and Full-Text Linking Technologies," discusses the important role played by library portals, particularly in relationship to simultaneous searching of multiple information resources and new full-text linking technologies.

This volume has been designed to provide 'deep background' to readers interested in better understanding some important new information technologies. It is our hope that this volume has identified issues that will play an important role in the lives of the science and technology librarian.

Mary C. Schlembach

Access to Remote Electronic Resources at the University of Arizona

Paul J. Bracke

SUMMARY. As libraries shift towards increasingly virtual collections, provision of both intellectual and physical or actual network access to an electronic resource is paramount to the ability of libraries to successfully serve customers. A number of issues make access to these resources difficult, including lack of persistence in the naming of resources and difficulties in providing remote access to resources. While it is impossible to absolutely control access within this electronic environment, it is possible to choose solutions that make managing access easier. The University of Arizona Libraries have chosen to use Persistent Uniform Resource Locators (PURLs) to address transience of links, and EZProxy, a pass-through proxy, to provide remote access as a solution to this problem. *[Article copies available for a fee from The Haworth Document Delivery Service: 1-800-HAWORTH. E-mail address: <getinfo@haworthpressinc.com> Website: <http://www.HaworthPress.com> © 2001 by The Haworth Press, Inc. All rights reserved.]*

KEYWORDS. Electronic resources, remote access, web catalogs, proxy servers

Paul J. Bracke is Systems Librarian, Main Library, University of Arizona, Tucson, AZ (E-mail: bracke@u.arizona.edu).

[Haworth co-indexing entry note]: "Access to Remote Electronic Resources at the University of Arizona." Bracke, Paul J. Co-published simultaneously in *Science & Technology Libraries* (The Haworth Information Press, an imprint of The Haworth Press, Inc.) Vol. 20, No. 2/3, 2001, pp. 5-14; and: *Electronic Resources and Services in Sci-Tech Libraries* (ed: Mary C. Schlembach, and William H. Mischo) The Haworth Information Press, an imprint of The Haworth Press, Inc., 2001, pp. 5-14. Single or multiple copies of this article are available for a fee from The Haworth Document Delivery Service [1-800-HAWORTH, 9:00 a.m. - 5:00 p.m. (EST). E-mail address: getinfo@haworthpressinc.com].

INTRODUCTION

The notion of what comprises a library collection has undergone a radical transformation over the past decade. In the past the collection was the sum of those physical objects owned and present in a particular location. Now the concept must also cover a more loosely defined amalgamation of resources accessible by members of an identifiable intellectual community. Libraries have been struggling with the implications of this change for the provision of access to electronic resources, as well as for the role of the catalog in organizing access. In order to be successful, it is essential for libraries to provide intellectual and physical access to remote collections in a consistent manner, regardless of a user's physical location. Unfortunately, a number of complications have made this a difficult issue.

Already overworked cataloging staff members have been overwhelmed by the quantity of new work and the new skills necessary to effectively manage electronic resources. The increasing availability of electronic resources has heightened demand on cataloging staff to keep the library catalog current. Steadily increasing numbers of resources are one reason for this, but certainly not the only. Electronic resources, particularly those on the Web, are often ephemeral in nature, and their restructuring or disappearance lead to frequent broken links and a new level of maintenance required for the catalog. In order to provide customers with a consistent manner of access to needed resources, policies and procedures must be formulated and enacted to assure systematic detection and repair of broken links, which introduces new work to cataloging staff and often requires new and different skills and knowledge on the part of staff.

The ability of a library to provide connectivity to remote resources, regardless of the user's physical location, is key to libraries providing even adequate service to customers in the electronic environment. Since many electronic resources are remote, the failure of remote authentication and authorization technologies to keep pace with the growing population of off-site users is problematic for libraries. Many existing authentication schemes employed by library vendors assume that users will be connected from a recognized network, or IP, address, generally located on a campus network. This is known as IP address validation, IP authentication, or IP filtering. Proxy servers, which allow off-site users to appear to vendors as coming from on-site, are a popular solution to this, but have shortcomings. Another, less frequently used, option is assignment of a User ID/Password combination.

Additionally, the library's traditional primary access point, the catalog, may be perceived as an obstacle to access. The catalog generally has higher requirements for effective use than many sites on the World Wide Web. Subject searching in the catalog, depending on the proper selection of subject headings, is difficult and confusing for users accustomed to clickable Web directories or keyword search engines. Some users also find catalog display formats difficult to understand, particularly in consortial environments. Perhaps most importantly, many catalogs do not, at least at this point, provide an easy mechanism for locating a desired resource through one or two clicks–a problem that can be circumvented by creating lists of resources on a library's Web page (Antelman 1999; Chrzastowski 1999).

While effective management of access to electronic resources is an important problem for all libraries, it has an especially large impact on science and technology libraries. Users of these libraries tend to rely on current journal literature, which increasingly is available in electronic format. For any library, providing access to resources, whether print or electronic, is the key to user success. Unlike the print environment of the past, physical location of a resource is no longer the key to access in the electronic environment. Although the physical location of a resource may now be irrelevant, the physical location of a user is not and is often specified by licensing agreements to restrict access to resources. This is especially important for users of science and technology libraries, some of whom may be located at satellite laboratories or facilities that can be difficult or inappropriate to include in campus IP ranges.

ACCESS TO E-RESOURCES

The World Wide Web has provided libraries with new alternatives for organizing access to resources, especially electronic ones. Organization of access to electronic resources is now being done through three methods, often used in combination with one another:

- Integration into the catalog
- Management of an electronic resources database separate from the catalog
- Management of static links on a library's website.

These methods, and a combination thereof, provide a balance between the user's need for easy access to resources and a library's need to maintain bibliographic control over its resources.

Many libraries have opted to provide access to electronic resources through the library's catalog. This reflects the idea that even in an electronic, networked environment, the catalog is still the central access mechanism for library resources. Cataloging of electronic resources also reflects an expanded notion of the library's collection to include resources that are neither owned nor physically housed at a library. Integration of electronic resources into the catalog usually is done by either creating separate records for electronic resources or by embedding a Uniform Resource Locator (URL) for electronic access in the 856 field of the MARC record for an existing print item, or both.

While there are certainly technical solutions to integrating records for electronic resources into the catalog, there are also some serious problems. As links are added to a catalog, their maintenance becomes an immediate issue. Checking for "dead" links can be a time-consuming task, even with link-checking software. Fixing them is not merely a matter of changing a URL in a catalog record. Someone must determine the new location of a resource, and possibly determine how to formulate a new URL that includes any necessary authentication or authorization information. At a minimum, these tasks require time, ingenuity, and persistence. Staff will also likely need new skills, and possibly new training.

Creating and maintaining records from aggregators of electronic information, especially electronic journal aggregators, are other time-consuming activities for technical services departments. At times, records for all titles in a collection are available from a vendor or another library and may be loaded in an automated manner into a library's catalog. More problematic are aggregators that frequently change title lists, or do not provide direct access to individual titles. This can make inclusion in the catalog almost impossible and mask access to potentially valuable resources.

Some libraries have opted to maintain separate databases or lists of electronic resources, especially electronic journals (Harker 1999; Mischo and Schlembach 1999). These databases and lists may or may not preclude the inclusion of records in the library's catalog. This result stems from concerns about the usability of web-based online catalogs; the ability of the current generation of catalogs to manage other information types relevant for administrative and/or access purposes, such as licensing information; and the interoperability of data stored in catalogs. These solutions do provide a method of presenting access to electronic resources in a manner that is integrated into the library's Web presence. However, creation of parallel systems to track electronic resources does have two potential weaknesses. First, it introduces the possibility of increased work as two databases of bibliographic information must be maintained. Some libraries have alleviated this problem by using a common database to generate lists of Web resources and MARC records for the catalog (Anderson 1999). Second, it increases the complexity of locating resources as intellectual access to a library's collection becomes segregated by material type. It may not be apparent, and probably is not convenient, for users to look in multiple locations to gain a comprehensive view of a library's relevant resources.

Regardless of which option a library chooses, the increasing number of electronic resources available to libraries makes their bibliographic control a monumental task. Even if free, non-licensed resources are excluded from the catalog, the number of licensed resources to be cataloged is daunting. The quantity of resources is constantly growing as more publishers make electronic versions of print texts available, as more back issues of journals or books are made available by publishers or through digitization projects, and as more electronic-only content becomes available.

To make organizing access to electronic resources easier the lack of permanent access must be addressed. Lack of permanence stems from a variety of causes, including the transitory nature of many Web resources and the mutability and lack of permanent naming conventions of URLs. While not much can be done about the transient nature of some content, the naming problem is something that can be addressed. Librarians hold out hope that a Uniform Resource Naming (URN) framework might emerge to solve this problem. URNs are intended to serve as persistent, location-independent resource identifiers (Connolly, accessed September 16, 2001). Although they are not in widespread use, URN-like name resolution services such as OCLC's Persistent Uniform Resource Locators (PURLs) exist, and are reliable and flexible (Weibel, accessed April 18, 2001). Other libraries, with locally-maintained databases of electronic resources, gain similar functionality by using local, permanently maintained scripts to redirect users to remote resources.

Unfortunately, provision of access to electronic resources is not just an issue of bibliographic description and access through the library's Web catalog and/or website. The current crude state of authentication and authorization on the Web has further complicated matters for libraries, which have found vendor-supported solutions (e.g., IP authentication) limiting and proxy servers difficult for users and sometimes inadequate in functionality.

PROVIDING REMOTE ACCESS TO ELECTRONIC RESOURCES

The increasing availability of electronic resources and the ever-expanding population of off-campus users have made the management of physical access to resources (i.e., being able to connect consistently, regardless of physical location) more difficult than ever. For science and technology libraries with a heavy emphasis on journal literature, this problem is especially acute, as these libraries are constantly increasing the number of electronic titles available to their customers. In some cases, print copies of journals are no longer available as libraries move to electronic-only subscriptions to facilitate cost-savings and greater desktop access (Krieb 1999).

Users expect access to campus resources, including library resources, from any location, just like any other Web resource. Unfortunately, access to remote, electronic resources licensed by libraries are almost always restricted in one of two ways: through IP address validation (i.e., a user must access a licensed resource from a recognized network address) or through a User ID/Password combination. IP-address validation is especially prevalent.

> Because IP filtering requires little maintenance, aggregators and publishers have adopted this form of access control, effectively shifting the onus of authentication to the subscribing library. As a result, many libraries must now be able to identify IP address information and the total number of computers associated with each subnet for their institution's network. To complicate this maintenance, some publishers require that the entire IP address be submitted for class B networks. For institutions using dynamic IP addressing, this information can be difficult to discern. (Krieb 1999)

Realizing that remote access is necessary for many users, libraries have employed a number of strategies for providing access to users not physically on, or connected to, campus. By far, the most common of these solutions, though not perfect, is the proxy server. Traditional proxy servers such as the Netscape Proxy Server, Microsoft Proxy Server, and Squid act essentially as forwarding services. They act as intermediaries between a user and remote Web sites, receiving requests from a user, making the request from the remote source, and passing it back to the user. These servers may have difficulties with some Web technologies that may be incorporated into remote resources that bypass proxied web connections. Such proxies also require reconfiguration of a user's browser, a task that is difficult for many users. Additional difficulties may be experienced because of firewalls and inconsistent behavior between browsers, especially as new browser versions are released. This can render even the best-written user instructions useless.

A solution gaining in popularity is the pass-through proxy. A pass-through proxy requires no browser configuration, just a modification of URLs to access-restricted resources. Essentially, links to proxied resources look identical to any other link on a library's website or in its catalog. A link to a pass-through proxy points a user to a proxy server, along with information on connecting the user to a desired resource (typically a URL). After the initial connection, at which point a user is authenticated against a file such as a campus database or catalog patron file, the proxy acts as a "broker." All requests are sent from user to proxy, which forwards the requests to the remote resource which in turn sees a valid IP address. The proxy rewrites the results from the remote resource for the user on the fly, so the user is always accessing the remote resource indirectly. Brown University has developed such solutions locally, while other libraries are deploying EZProxy, a commercial solution (Goerwitz 1998). The popular Apache server also includes a module to facilitate this functionality.

While all proxies work reasonably well, and rewriting proxies increase the ease of use for remote users, they still fall short of the ideal solution for providing access to remote users. Ideally, users would be able to authenticate against a central authentication service and then have direct, rather than proxied, access to a resource. This would require trust of authentication between organizations (e.g., a university and a vendor), and require libraries or their parent organization to have a means of authenticating all users. Projects such as the Internet2's Shibboleth project are promising steps in this direction (Shibboleth Project 2001).

THE ARIZONA SOLUTION

The University of Arizona Library has chosen to provide access to electronic resources through its catalog, in addition to listings of databases on its website. Naming issues are being addressed through the implementation of Persistent URLs (PURLs). Remote access is currently being transitioned to EZProxy, a pass-through proxy, though likely only an interim solution.

Electronic journals and books are, for the most part, included in the catalog. The library uses catalog records from vendors or other sources wherever possible as a source of cataloging information for large aggregations of titles. Abstracting and indexing services and other databases are generally accessible only through the library's website, although some have also been included in the library catalog.

The Web is still a volatile environment, and no solution to manage distributed resources can be perfect at this point in time. What is possible, however, is to choose a solution that is reasonably reliable now, that can be moved into the future either by software vendors or by migrating data, and that can be supported by the staff at a given institution. The University of Arizona Library is working towards such a solution.

The naming problem is being addressed through the implementation of a Persistent Uniform Resource Locator (PURL) server. The PURL server acts as a URL resolution service for users. Using a Web interface based on simple HTML forms, library staff assign a PURL to a resource. To an end user, a PURL looks like any other URL. For example, a PURL for BIOSIS might be: http://purl.library.arizona.edu/dbs/biosis. This PURL would then be used throughout the library's website and in the library catalog. Anytime a user clicked on the PURL, a request would be sent to the PURL server, which would redirect the user to the appropriate address (Weibel, accessed April 18, 2001).

A PURL would be used in the catalog and on library Web pages instead of the direct URL. So, if BIOSIS were linked to on 15 pages and in the library catalog, all links could be updated through the changing of a single PURL, instead of in 16 places. Once created, librarians or other staff members who maintain the catalog or library webpages would be able to search the central PURL registry for the proper name. As Maggie Farrell put it:

> PURLs have significant implications for online catalogs. The maintenance of URLs within online catalogs, especially those with a Web interface, is often time consuming and overwhelming for local catalogers. When one reflects on all of the catalogers trying to maintain thousands of URLs within catalogs, it boggles the mind of the effort required to keep local catalogs current. (Farrell 1999)

While PURLs are only as effective and reliable as the maintenance that goes into them, "PURLs increase the probability of correct resolution and thereby reduce the burden and expense of catalog maintenance" (Weibel).

PURLs can be used not only to reduce the labor of catalog and website maintenance, but to also redirect users to the appropriate address. In cases where information about a proxy server, or other remote access solution, can be encoded in a URL, a PURL could be used to direct users to a proxied version of a licensed resource. EZProxy, a pass-through proxy solution, offers such an encoding using a prefix to reflect an institution's proxy server, as well as a parameter with the user's target URL. Since users from campus IP addresses (i.e., non-restricted addresses) are ignored by EZProxy, a PURL can be constructed to point to the version of a remote resource (i.e., proxied or non-proxied) that is appropriate for the user.

For example, the University of Arizona's EZProxy server is located at: http://ezproxy.library.arizona.edu/. To construct a proxied link to the library catalog <http://sabio.library.arizona.edu>, one would write a link that looks like: http://ezproxy.library.arizona.edu/login?url=http://sabio.library. arizona.edu. If a PURL, such as <http://purl.library.arizona.edu/sabio> were then created to resolve to the above URL, a single PURL could be presented to users through the catalog and library's Web page that would provide persistent access to authorized users, regardless of location, so long as the PURL is maintained. Although maintenance is not eliminated, it is centralized and generally reduced.

CONCLUSION

As libraries shift towards increasingly virtual collections, provision of both intellectual and physical or actual network access to an electronic resource is paramount to the ability of libraries to successfully serve customers. A number of issues make access to these resources difficult, including: lack of persistence in the naming of resources, lack of persistence in resources, the expanding universe of electronic information (most of which is not owned or physically possessed by a library), and difficulties in providing remote access to resources.

While all of these issues (as well as others) are important, it is impossible to address them all simultaneously, so libraries must choose which issues to target. The University of Arizona Libraries have chosen two vehicles for providing access: the library website for databases, and the catalog for electronic journals and books. For the most part a resource is in one place or the other, but there are exceptions. For example, subject selectors will sometimes supplement catalog access with a page of electronic journals in a given aggregation or subject (e.g., all American Chemical Society Journals are listed at: http://dizzy.library.arizona. edu/library/teams/set/e-journal_pages/acs.html).

Although it is impossible to prevent electronic resources from changing URLs, or disappearing altogether, it is possible to make the management of URLs a centralized task. By providing a central point, such as a PURL server, for management of links, libraries can quickly respond to change no matter where links to electronic resources are provided. The University of Arizona Library has elected to address this using PURLs.

Providing remote access to library resources is a problem all libraries have grappled with, but that has not been addressed to the complete satisfaction of librarians, vendors, and most importantly, customers. Traditional and pass-through proxies have shortcomings, although pass-through proxies have a number of compelling advantages, particularly in ease-of-use for the customer to make them a reasonable solution to remote access. Ultimately, any proxy solution should not be a long term remote access solution: new trust systems should be developed so users can authenticate with their home institution and then have a direct connection to the vendor.

REFERENCES

Anderson, Barbara. 1999. Web lists or OPACs: can we have our cake and eat it, too? *Library Computing* 18(4):312-316.

Antelman, Kristin. 1999. Web lists and the decline of the library catalog. *Library Computing* 18(3):189-195.

Chrzastowski, Tina E. 1999. E-journal access: the online catalog (856 field), Web lists, and "The principle of least effort." *Library Computing* 18(4):317-322.

Connolly, Dan. "Naming and Addressing: URIs, URLs, . . . " Available at: <http://www.w3.org/Addressing/> (accessed September 16, 2001).

Farrell, Maggie. 1999. URLs and PURLs. *DttP* 27(2):4-5.

Goerwitz, Richard. 1998. Pass-through proxying as a solution to the off-site web-access problem. *D-Lib Magazine*, Available at: <http://www.dlib.org/dlib/june98/stg/06goerwitz.html>.

Harker, Karen. 1999. Order out of chaos: using a web database to manage access to electronic journals at the University of Texas Southwestern Medical Center. *Library Computing* 18(1):59-67.

Krieb, Dennis. 1999. You can't get there from here: Issues in remote access to electronic journals for a Health Sciences Library. *Issues in Science and Technology Librarianship*. Available at: <http://www.library.ucsb.edu/istl/99-spring/article3.html>.

Mischo, William H. and Mary C. Schlembach. 1999. Web-based access to locally developed databases. *Library Software Review*. 18(1,2):51-59.

Shibboleth Project. Shibboleth Project Home Page. Available at: <http://middleware.internet2.edu/shibboleth/> (accessed May 29, 2001).

Weibel, Stu, Erik Jul, and Keith Shafer. PURLs: Persistent Uniform Resource Locators. Available at: <http://purl.oclc.org/OCLC/PURL/summary> (accessed April 18, 2001).

Providing Access to Online Government Documents in an Academic Research Library Collection: A Case Study in the Geosciences

Kristi L. Jensen

SUMMARY. This article provides an overview of the move to online federal government documents and the problems associated with maintaining access to government documents in the online environment. In addition, the impact of the shift to online government documents on an academic research library collection in the geosciences is examined by assessing whether or not items from one publication series of the U.S. Geological Survey are included in several traditional library research tools. The results of this analysis and some recommendations for dealing with hidden online government documents are also discussed. *[Article copies available for a fee from The Haworth Document Delivery Service: 1-800-HAWORTH. E-mail address: <getinfo@haworthpressinc.com> Website: <http://www.HaworthPress.com> © 2001 by The Haworth Press, Inc. All rights reserved.]*

KEYWORDS. Online government documents, government publications–distribution and acquisition, earth science libraries, geoscience libraries, federal depository library program, U.S. geological survey

Kristi L. Jensen, MLS, is Assistant Librarian, Fletcher L. Byrom Earth and Mineral Sciences Library, Pennsylvania State University, University Park, PA.

[Haworth co-indexing entry note]: "Providing Access to Online Government Documents in an Academic Research Library Collection: A Case Study in the Geosciences." Jensen, Kristi L. Co-published simultaneously in *Science & Technology Libraries* (The Haworth Information Press, an imprint of The Haworth Press, Inc.) Vol. 20, No. 2/3, 2001, pp. 15-25; and: *Electronic Resources and Services in Sci-Tech Libraries* (ed: Mary C. Schlembach, and William H. Mischo) The Haworth Information Press, an imprint of The Haworth Press, Inc., 2001, pp. 15-25. Single or multiple copies of this article are available for a fee from The Haworth Document Delivery Service [1-800-HAWORTH, 9:00 a.m. - 5:00 p.m. (EST). E-mail address: getinfo@haworthpressinc.com].

INTRODUCTION

Academic researchers and librarians in the sciences know that government documents are an essential part of a research library collection. As Cheverie points out, "Federal information plays an important role in achieving the mission of research and education institutions" (Cheverie 1998). Given recent changes in the world of government documents, however, research libraries are struggling with issues that will determine how well government information is represented in their collections in the future.

Recent federal legislation has encouraged the use of the Internet as a repository for government documents and necessitated an increase in the publication of online government documents by many federal agencies (Souza and Dodsworth 1998). This shift in format poses both challenges and opportunities for libraries that have typically collected government information. As Sheehy and Sevetson indicate "the success of the modern depository program rests in the depository libraries' ability to provide resources and support for electronic information" (Sheehy and Sevetson 1999).

Since the advent of the Internet, librarians have been dealing with the access issues that arise in the online environment (Laskowski 2000). While the number of online publications remained relatively small, at least compared to the volume of physical materials still available, librarians focused attention on a number of important issues. For example, depository libraries examined whether or not they had the appropriate hardware and software needed to access online and other digital materials, thereby ensuring equity of access to government materials. In addition, other questions were raised about how best to integrate new formats into existing library collections, how to guarantee that online documents were authentic and had not been changed from the original, and finally, who was now responsible for guaranteeing that online resources would remain permanently available.

The number of online government documents continues to increase exponentially each year with a parallel increase in the number of documents available exclusively in an online format. The Government Accounting Office (GAO) report entitled "Information Management: Electronic Dissemination of Government Publications" purports that the "electronic dissemination of government documents offers the opportunity to reduce the costs of dissemination and make government information more usable and accessible" (GAO 2001). This belief, that online government documents are more accessible to all users of government information, has yet to be proven.

It is true that users from many different geographic locations can *potentially* access an online government document compared to a physical copy in a depository library. Whether or not users can *actually* access an online document is dependent on a number of variables. The GAO report mentioned above also points out that "even frequent Internet users may find it difficult to search for and locate specific government documents on the Web" (GAO 2001). In addition, a "Comprehensive Assessment of Public Information Dissemination" report from the National Commission on Libraries and Information Science (NCLIS) indicates that information literacy skills, as well as the appropriate technology, are required to provide both intellectual and physical access to online documents (NCLIS 2001). In short, placing a document on a government website does not ensure access to that resource.

Another roadblock to increased access occurs if it is assumed that the traditional method of distributing government documents is adequate for the online environment. The GAO report on Electronic Dissemination specifically states that the Government Printing Office's (GPO) ability to acquire and disseminate government documents has already been impaired. "In 1996, GPO estimated that about 50 percent of government documents published in that year were not indexed, catalogued, and distributed to depository libraries" (GAO 2001).

Why is it so difficult for the GPO to "disseminate" online documents to depository libraries? One of the primary reasons online documents are unavailable is the dependence of the GPO on the publishing agencies to notify them of the existence of these documents (GPO 1996). As Stierholz pointed out in the early days of online government documents, "As each federal agency provides online documents, it becomes more difficult to impose organization on the information" (Stierholz 1996). One step in this organizational process includes the dissemination of documents by the GPO to depository libraries. Hernon and Relyea emphasize that "as agencies produce electronic products and services, there are increased opportunities to bypass the GPO and its depository program and to communicate directly to the public" (Hernon and Relyea 1995). A more dispersed network environment that allows publishing agencies to bypass the traditional reporting mechanisms means that some resources may never be included in library catalogs or online indexes, the tools frequently used in an academic research library to provide access to government information.

Thus, rather than becoming more accessible these *undistributed* online documents may become almost entirely inaccessible to the typical user in a large research library. One of the values of integrating government documents into a research collection is the opportunity for researchers to happen across these materials while browsing the shelves or searching for keywords and concepts in various databases, including an online catalog. Many users find government documents in library collections utilizing these search strategies. If an online document has not been cataloged and *added* to the collection or indexed in one of the subject specific databases, users may never have the opportunity to find it even if it is pertinent to their research.

Despite the Federal Depository Library Program's (FDLP) Information Dissemination and Access Strategic Plan to deal with changes in the current federal dissemination program, many online government documents appear to be slipping through the cracks (GPO 1996). Instead of providing greater access to government documents, the publishing of online documents may be hindering access to these resources. Yott points out that "the burden has fallen on libraries to develop mechanisms and procedures to ensure that the information distributed remains useful and accessible" (Yott 1998). Given the importance of government publications in a research library collection and the current state of affairs with the FDLP, the question arises, how can we as managers of large research collections make sure that users are gaining access to this rather ephemeral material?

ONLINE GOVERNMENT DOCUMENTS AND THE GEOSCIENCES

Background

In order to more clearly understand the impact of online government publications on a research library's ability to provide access to these materials, a case study in the geosciences was undertaken. The geosciences provide an opportune area of study for several reasons. First, the United States Geological Survey (USGS) publishes a profuse number of government publications heavily utilized by researchers in the geosciences. As Haner noted, ". . . geological research depends to a considerable extent upon government documents" (Haner 1989). In addition, the USGS has demonstrated a propensity for online publishing. Thousands of documents are already available from a variety of web sites and a number of lists of available electronic publications are maintained. Also, the USGS is a decentralized agency composed of numerous divisions, departments and offices with physical locations across the U.S. Providing coherent and consistent access to online materials in this distributed environment is an important measure of an agency's ability to report and disseminate online materials. Finally, the publications of the USGS have historically been integrated into a wide variety of research tools, including online library catalogs and subject specific databases. A variety of these tools could be examined in order to determine how well online government documents have been represented in each.

This investigation was prompted by the serendipitous discovery that the Fletcher L. Byrom Earth and Mineral Sciences Library collection at The Pennsylvania State University lacked many USGS publications that were readily available online. These missing items included publications that would normally have been received as part of the Federal Depository Library Program. In order to facilitate the inclusion of these hidden resources in our collection, a list was compiled indicating online documents that needed to be added to or linked from our library catalog. The initial list of publications (List A–see Figure 1) was compiled from the USGS list of online publications (available at http://geology.usgs. gov/books.html). The initial research included a variety of publication series available from the USGS, for example, bulletins, circulars, open-file reports, etc. However, given the mass of available online publications a decision was made to focus initial research on one series, the open-file reports. According to the USGS web site (http://pubs.usgs.gov/products/ books/), open-file reports include "unpublished manuscript reports, maps, and other materials that are made available for public consultation at depositories."

The open-file report series was chosen for a number of reasons. First, our collection seemed to be missing a large number of these informal publications. Despite the informal nature of these publications they are frequently used and often contain information that is never published anywhere else. Second, these reports should have been added to our collection as part of our federal depository receipts. The Pennsylvania State University Libraries are an 80% depository and have chosen to receive the USGS open-file reports as part of this program. Given the fact that we should have been receiving these documents on a regular basis, it was important to find out exactly what we were missing. Third, our collection typically included open-file reports on microfiche. Given negative user reaction to the microfiche format, the provision of an alternative online format was deemed extremely attractive. Finally, the number of yearly publications in this series is large. By dealing with one of the larger publication series, the extent of the impact of online publishing on the creation of "fugitive" documents, those not distributed in accord with federal stat-utes, could be more clearly assessed.

Various processes were implemented to "discover" hidden online open-file reports. The USGS list of online documents supplied a number of servers or web sites providing online documents. While exploring some of the USGS servers providing access to online resources, docu-ments that were not included on the USGS online publications website were discovered. Each site was explored and missing items were identi-fied. In addition, a variety of other search mechanisms were utilized to find online open-file reports. Searches were performed using FirstGov (http://www.firstgov.gov), the USGS search engine (http://www.usgs. gov), Google's Uncle Sam site (http://www.google.com/unclesam) and the Search Adobe PDF Online site (http://searchpdf.adobe.com/). In the end a comprehensive list of online USGS open-file reports was produced (List B–see Figure 1) including items listed on the USGS list of online publications (List A) and items discovered using the search processes mentioned above.

The initial purpose of the project was to create broader access to online government documents by adding links to catalog records referencing a document in another format and by adding records for online documents that had never been included in our collection. Over time a broader goal was developed, ensuring that students and faculty had access to these on-line government resources from multiple access points typically used in the research process. Further analysis was completed in order to deter-mine how well hidden these documents really were.

Results

By comparing the comprehensive list of online open-file reports with the online catalog, 760 online documents were identified as additions to our collection. In addition, 308 records required the addition of a link to an existing catalog record. Besides these simple updates and additions, some records requiring maintenance were identified and procedures for entering linking information in these records were standardized. In the end, over 1300 items were included on the comprehensive list of online open-file reports (List B) and were evaluated for inclusion in or addition to our collection.

While it is significant that over 760 items readily available online were missing from our collection, it is more important to note that over 240 of these items were not listed on the USGS list of online open-file reports. If a library depended on the USGS list of reports as the definitive source of information for online reports within the agency, approximately 30% of the items available online in this series would be invisible. This set of 240 items, missing from both our catalog and the USGS list of reports, became the working group of items searched for in other library resources (List C–see Figure 1).

GeoRef, the premier online geosciences database, was searched for each of the 240 missing reports. Approximately half of the missing items were not found in GeoRef. A portion of the items not found in GeoRef may be accounted for by their recent publication dates, 2000 and 2001. If the 2000 and 2001 documents were eliminated from evaluation, approximately 49 of the remaining 155 documents were absent from GeoRef. If a researcher was searching for a particular concept, s/he would have no

FIGURE 1. Summary of Lists

List A: **USGS List of Online Open File Reports**
(http://pubs.usgs.gov/products/books/openfile/)

List B: **Comprehensive List of Online Open File Reports =**
USGS List of Online Open File Reports +
Additional Online Open File Reports discovered
on USGS servers   (approximately 1300 items)

List C: **Final working group of documents to search**
for in other library tools =
Items from List B missing from both the PSU Library
Catalog and from List A–the USGS List of Online
Open File Reports (240 items)

chance of locating these 240 documents in our catalog and would find only half of these items in GeoRef. Even more significant is the fact that only one of the items located in GeoRef had a link to the online version of the publication. Therefore, even if a library user found one of the missing items in the database, she would still come up empty-handed when she turned to our catalog to see if the library owned that item. Even locating a reference in GeoRef would not effectively lead a researcher to the item unless our catalog were updated to include these missing materials.

Another question also needed to be addressed: How widespread was the problem of the missing document? In other words, were we the only organization lacking access to these materials or was a similar phenomenon occurring in other academic research libraries? In order to better answer this question, two peer institution library catalogs with itemized holdings of open-file reports were identified and searched to determine if the missing items appeared in their catalogs in any format. Both institutions were comparable depository libraries and include online materials in their catalogs. Both institutions' catalogs contained records for the print or microfiche version of 36 of the 240 missing items. Of these 36 items only two had links to the online version of the report. Not only were these 240 missing items invisible to users via our online catalog, but a majority of these items were also missing from the collections of similar academic libraries.

In addition to examining the catalogs of individual institutions, a search of OCLC's WorldCat was completed to see if the 240 missing items were available in other library settings. A WorldCat search produced 761 items to compare with the missing items list (List C). Of the 240 missing items, only 51 were cataloged in WorldCat as online documents. Almost all of the 51 items found in WorldCat were available in only 2 libraries. When the libraries holding these materials were examined more closely, they were typically USGS or other governmental libraries, not academic research libraries. Once again, the 240 missing items remained well hidden.

Another resource, the Catalog of U.S. Publications, was searched to determine whether or not the missing reports could be found using this important federal resource. According to the Catalog of U.S. Publications website (http://www.access.gpo.gov/su_docs/locators/cgp/), this resource can be used to "link to Federal agency online resources or identify materials distributed to Federal Depository Libraries." Although researchers might not typically be referred to this resource during the research process, determining whether or not the Catalog could be used as a collection development tool to find items missing from our collection was important. Additionally, given the fact that items appearing in the Catalog could be uploaded into our collection as part of future Marcive updates, now set to include online resources, time searching for fugitive documents could be saved if the documents could be found here. Rather than searching for any record correlating to the missing documents, only records with links to the online document were sought. Only 4 records were found that matched items on the missing open-file report list. Once again, almost all of the missing documents remain hidden when using this resource (see Figure 2).

CONCLUSIONS AND RECOMMENDATIONS

In the end, every library resource evaluated failed to find a majority of the missing online documents. If the state of online documents available from the USGS is any indicator of the general status of all federal documents, there is much cause for concern. Almost 30% of the documents examined remain hidden no matter which resource is utilized to find these items. Despite the fact that 240 missing items were identified, these results were produced only after hours of searching. Most libraries cannot afford to spend an exhaustive amount of time searching for missing on-line documents. Although the searching was thorough, more missing reports are still out there. It is impossible to say that any search for these resources has been comprehensive. At the same time, a library collection can no longer be considered complete without the inclusion of online government documents (Souza and Dodsworth 1998).

FIGURE 2. Number of Items from List C Found in Various Research Tools

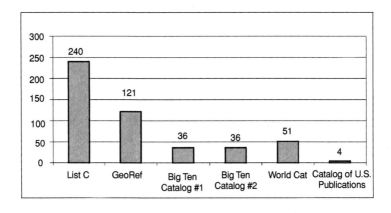

Given the decentralized nature of agencies like the USGS and the current reporting structure within the FDLP, it is unlikely they will be able to ensure that their online publications are linked from their online publications list or reported to the GPO. As Jobe recently pointed out "The Internet has strained distribution programs and business models that were originally designed in the 19th and 20th centuries" (Jobe 2001). The FDLP Information Dissemination and Access Strategic Plan: 1996-2001 was intended to deal with the problem of online publishing and dissemination but has had very little effect (GPO 1996). As Brown indicates, "a measure of enforcement is needed to ensure that agencies comply with statutory requirements . . . No form of punishment exists to force agencies to follow the specifications of Title 44" (Brown 1999). Hidden online government documents can be expected to remain a problem for the developers of academic research library collections until a more effective and comprehensive government policy dealing with the dissemination of online documents has been both crafted and implemented.

The recent NCLIS report to Congress provides numerous recommendations for the restructuring of the traditional dissemination process for federal government publications. Only time will tell whether these recommendations will be implemented and prove to be more effective than previous attempts. Given the current circumstances, a limited amount of time to spend locating missing online government documents, inadequate distribution of these resources via traditional depository mechanisms, and the need to include these important materials in a research collection, librarians find themselves in a seemingly unsolvable predicament. During this time of transition, several strategies can be implemented by librarians and other information professionals to alleviate these conditions and encourage the move to a more successful reporting and dissemination process. Librarians can:

- monitor and participate in the ongoing discussion related to the future of the Federal Depository Library Program and plans for the future "dissemination" of online government documents.
- encourage the publishers of federal information to implement more effective procedures, including statements of accountability, for tracking all publications within their agency, department, or division.
- provide for the integration of "found" online government documents into existing library tools, e.g., online library catalogs and subject specific resources.
- share information about "missing" documents with the publishing agency and other research libraries.

REFERENCES

Brown, Wendy R. 1999. Federal initiatives to promote access to electronic government information: the impact on the federal depository library program. *Law Library Journal* 91 (2):291-303.

Cheverie, Joan F. 1998. Access to and services for federal information in the networked environment: Institutional issues and strategies. *Journal of Academic Librarianship* 24 (5):392-394.

Haner, Barbara E. 1989. The use of government documents by geologists as cited in the geologic literature from a circulation study in a geology branch library. In *Proceedings of the Twenty-Third Meeting of the Geoscience Information Society,* ed. Joanne V. Lerud, Denver.

Hernon, Peter and Harold C. Relyea. Government publishing: Past to present. *Government Information Quarterly* 12 (3):314-330.

Jobe, Margaret M. 2001. Government information at a crossroads. *Library Journal* 126 (9):62-66.

Laskowski, Mary Schneider. 2000. The impact of electronic access to government information: What users and document specialists think. *Journal of Government Information* 27 (2):173-185.

Sheehy, Helen M. and Andrea Sevetson. 1999. International information update: Preparing Canada for a digital world. *Journal of Government Information* 26 (2):165-170.

Souza, Jennifer L. and Ellen M. Dodsworth. 1998. Government information today: The dilemma of digital collections. *Collection Management* 23 (3):21-31.

Stierholz, Katrina. 1996. U.S. government documents in the electronic era: Problems and promise. *Collection Management* 21 (1):41-56.

U.S. General Accounting Office (GAO). 2001. Information Management: Electronic Dissemination of Government Publications. Washington, D.C. (http://www.gao.gov/new.items/d01428.pdf).

U.S. Government Printing Office (GPO). 1996. Study to Identify Measures Necessary for a Successful Transition to a More Electronic Federal Depository Library Program. Washington, D.C.: U.S. Government Printing Office. (Exhibit 1 is the strategic plan).

U.S. National Commission on Libraries and Information Science (NCLIS). 2001. A Comprehensive Assessment of Public Information Dissemination, Final Report, Volume 1. Washington, D.C.: U.S. Government Printing Office.

Yott, Patrick. Enhancing access to government information: Redistribution of data via the world wide web. *Collection Management* 23 (3): 61-76.

Publishing Mathematics on the Web

Timothy W. Cole

SUMMARY. The World Wide Web is an invaluable tool for communicating scholarly information, but there remain difficulties and issues when trying to use the Web to communicate certain kinds of information, notably scholarly journal articles containing complex mathematics. This paper looks at some of these concerns and the approaches being used today to address them. Illustrations are drawn from the Illinois Digital Library Journal Article Testbed that currently contains over 65,000 online journal articles in the disciplines of physics and engineering. The latest developments in the use of MathML on the Web are discussed. *[Article copies available for a fee from The Haworth Document Delivery Service: 1-800-HAWORTH. E-mail address: <getinfo@haworthpressinc.com> Website: <http://www.HaworthPress.com> © 2001 by The Haworth Press, Inc. All rights reserved.]*

KEYWORDS. Mathematics on the Web, MathML, PDF, T_EX, OpenMath

INTRODUCTION

In 1978 Donald Knuth, while still in the throes of creating the now ubiquitous mathematics authoring and typesetting standard T_EX, delivered the Josiah Williard Gibbs Lecture on the topic of "Mathematical Typography" (Knuth 1979). He suggested that typography, when considered "as the ser-

---

Timothy W. Cole, MLS, is Mathematics Librarian and Associate Professor of Library Administration, University of Illinois at Urbana-Champaign, Urbana, IL.

[Haworth co-indexing entry note]: "Publishing Mathematics on the Web." Cole, Timothy W. Co-published simultaneously in *Science & Technology Libraries* (The Haworth Information Press, an imprint of The Haworth Press, Inc.) Vol. 20, No. 2/3, 2001, pp. 27-44; and: *Electronic Resources and Services in Sci-Tech Libraries* (ed: Mary C. Schlembach, and William H. Mischo) The Haworth Information Press, an imprint of The Haworth Press, Inc., 2001, pp. 27-44. Single or multiple copies of this article are available for a fee from The Haworth Document Delivery Service [1-800-HAWORTH, 9:00 a.m. - 5:00 p.m. (EST). E-mail address: getinfo@haworthpressinc.com].

27

vant of mathematics," should have as a goal "to communicate mathematics effectively by making it possible to publish mathematical papers and books of high quality, without excessive cost." His vision, articulated before the introduction of the personal computer and more than a decade before the World Wide Web was launched, foreshadowed a primary function of the Web today. Conceived of initially as an improved way for high-energy physicists to collaborate, the Web has become an invaluable tool for communicating scholarly information. Unfortunately, achieving the desired quality of presentation isn't automatic when communicating certain kinds of information via the Web. Notably there are difficulties and issues that arise when using today's Web-enabled applications to display documents that include complex mathematics.

The difficulties when trying to present mathematics on the Web stem from a combination of circumstances. The syntax and notation of mathematics have always been challenging to render in a clear and unequivocal manner. The objective of conventional mathematical notation is "to be compact and to be understood by a reader who is aware of the conventions in force in each document" (Carlisle 2000). Written mathematics employs a wide range of special fonts, characters, arrangements, and alignments to express meaning. There is often more than one way to represent the same mathematical concept. Similar constructs may be used to communicate different meanings, and new symbols and forms of expression are added routinely as new mathematical concepts are developed and refined. The language of mathematics is dynamic and demanding to represent in any medium.

At the same time, most authors and available authoring tools still optimize for print media rather than electronic. In writing for print publications authors are concerned first with describing the appearance of the mathematics. While some print-based technologies have been adapted for use on the Web, such approaches have inherent limitations. Francis Wright points out that such formats "are excellent for printed documents, and range from good to acceptable for static documents to be accessed via the Web, but (roughly speaking) the less similar to HTML a format is the poorer it is for dynamic documents" (Wright 2000). Entirely new technologies, optimized for describing mathematics in a digital environment, are beginning to emerge, but these technologies diverge from print-based approaches and the prerequisite rendering capabilities are not always available on end-user workstations.

Because there is as yet no "best way" to implement mathematics for the generic Web environment, it remains difficult to select an approach for a particular application. The optimum choice depends not only on the scope and complexity of the content, but also on the nature of the rendering tools available to the intended audience, the context of the implementation, and the anticipated way in which the mathematics will be used. Is the primary object to emulate an existing, static print document exactly (e.g., down to the page structure and typography of the printed version)? How thoroughly must the math be integrated with surrounding text? Is the mathematics to be used directly (i.e., be interactive)? There are approaches available now or becoming available soon that address these issues individually but interoperability among the various approaches remains poor.

This paper begins with a brief enumeration of some of the difficulties inherent in the composition of mathematics for both printed page and screen. Web-specific approaches, adaptations of print-optimized approaches, and recent developments in semantic math initiatives are then discussed and categorized. Illustrations are drawn from the Illinois Digital Library Journal Article Testbed project (described in detail elsewhere, e.g., Schatz et al. 1999, Mischo and Cole 2000, Cole et al. 2001). The Illinois Testbed, created in 1994, currently contains over 65,000 online journal articles in multiple digital formats from more than 50 academic journals and handbooks in physics and engineering. This collection of articles contains many examples of high-level, complex mathematics. Some individual Testbed articles contain more than 1,000 instances of mathematical expressions.

FUNDAMENTAL ISSUES AND CHOICES

Typically, mathematical expressions are interspersed with explanatory narrative. In his book on mathematical typography Steven Krantz points out, "An important decision, which the mathematical author must make frequently and effectively, is whether to display a mathematical expression [separate it vertically from text before and after using white space] or leave it inline" (Krantz 2001). In making such decisions authors and editors are trained to take into account a wide range of factors–e.g., length of the mathematical expression relative to printed page line length, how near the end of a printed line an expression will occur (i.e., the risk of a line break in the middle of the expression), the effect inline setting of an expression will have on line leading, and the complexity and importance of the expression.

Those authoring or editing for the Web must adapt such criteria to take into account additional factors unique to the Web environment. For instance, the line length of an HTML or XML document is typically determined by the browser window width and is not meaningfully controllable (or knowable a priori) by the author. This eliminates the usefulness of line length in determining whether an expression should be displayed or presented inline. On the other hand, "no break" style instructions can be used in both Hypertext Markup Language (HTML) and Extensible Markup Language (XML) to obviate the concern about a line break in the wrong place in an expression. (Horizontal scroll bars appear as needed.) End-users also ultimately control font size in HTML and XML displays. This makes mathematical expressions that have been formatted as embedded graphics (e.g., GIF, JPEG, or PNG figures) stand out badly, especially when positioned inline. Finally, some of the built-in optimizations available in print are not always available on the Web. Print page optimized typesetting systems like T_EX differentiate between inline and display versions of the same expression. Thus the expression $\sum_{j=1}^{10} a_j$ inline becomes

$$\sum_{j=1}^{10} a_j$$

when presented as display mathematics. The first version of the expression, though it still impacts line leading, is more appropriate for inline use than the second version of the same (mathematically speaking) expression. Most currently available HTML and XML rendering engines aren't sophisticated enough to automatically optimize in this way for inline and display presentations. This complicates translation of print documents to HTML or XML.

There are other choices of notation and representation that can exacerbate rendering and presentation issues in a Web environment. Most notations that cause rendering problems in print tend to cause even greater problems when rendered for the Web. Recommended cautions regarding choice of notations for print (e.g., see Krantz 2001, pp. 3-11, 111) should be followed when authoring for the Web. For instance, an effort should be made to minimize stacking of accents, nesting of superscripts and subscripts, over-stretching of radical signs, accents, and fences, etc. These types of excesses in notation are hard to render accurately in print and even harder to render well in a Web browser window.

Finally, fonts and glyphs used in advanced mathematics can be especially troublesome when authoring for the Web. In the print environment, it is incumbent upon the author and publisher to negotiate font issues, but once negotiated, the ink is committed to paper and the issue has been dealt with. Not so in an online environment, at least not always.

A few online formats, notably Adobe's Portable Document Format (PDF), do embed all font sets required to render an article (as a result PDF files can be quite large), but most other formats, including T_EX (and Device Independent [DVI] files derived from T_EX document instances), do not. (T_EX files include the identity of the fonts needed, but not the actual font sets or subsets required.) While it's possible to embed font sets in HTML and XML (fonts are actually transmitted as separate files in a manner transparent to the end-user), the process is laborious and problematic, especially when trying to ensure proper rendering on multiple platforms (e.g., Windows, Macintosh, UNIX), and is done differently on different versions of Web browsers. Permission of intellectual property owners also may be required before embedding certain fonts in HTML and XML files. Embedded font information can be overridden by the end-user. By default, HTML and XML documents do not embed fonts, leaving decisions about fonts (and substitution for unavailable fonts) up to the client system.

Recognizing the significance of font issues in a Web environment, STIPUB (Scientific and Technical Information Publishers), a group that includes Elsevier Science, the American Institute of Physics, the American Physical Society, the American Mathematical Society, and the Institute of Electrical Engineers, initiated the STIX project (http://www.ams.org/STIX/) in 1997. Working with other interested parties (e.g., the W3 Consortium's MathML Working Group) the STIX project drafted a proposal for incorporating additional mathematical alphanumeric and technical symbols in the Unicode Standard. Unicode (which in its phase 1 implementation allows for the definition of more than 64,000 distinct characters) has become the recommended way to deal with font issues in HTML and XML. The Unicode Technical Committee has ratified the STIX proposal (with minor changes) and provisional code points have been assigned. The STIX project is now committed to developing (and making available for use without cost) scalable glyphs for the complete set of mathematic and technical characters in Unicode. Once this work has been completed and distribution of it becomes widespread, fonts and font sets will be much less of a concern for Web authors and publishers of documents containing mathematical content.

MATH AS EMBEDDED IMAGES IN HTML DOCUMENTS

Earlier versions of HTML were especially limited in terms of advanced typography and page (screen) composition. Mechanisms to include non-ASCII characters in HTML (beyond a handful of pre-defined entities–e.g., © for the copyright symbol) were cumbersome and often relied on the use of specific font sets, which might or might not be present on client workstations. Non-standard text alignment beyond simple superscript and subscript was not easily done using HTML prior to version 4 and the approximately concurrent introduction of Cascading Style Sheets (CSS). Use of combining diacritics was not supported. In this early Web environment rendering of mathematical content directly in HTML was problematic and the chance that a given end-user would see what the author intended him or her to see was low.

Given these limitations, GIF or JPEG images embedded in the HTML were frequently used to render mathematics of even minimal complexity. Such images of mathematical expressions could be generated in a variety of ways, ranging from the manual capture of screen renderings in popular document authoring systems to automated conversion of encoded equation fragments to image files (e.g., using Microsoft Word's built-in HTML tools or the L^AT_EX2HTML freeware utility). While this approach created its own set of formatting problems and reduced meaningful integration of mathematics in the delivered document, at least authors knew more reliably what the mathematics would look like to the end-user.

This approach is still widely used today, with the PNG image format having been added as an alternative to GIF and JPEG formats. Figure 1 illustrates the use of embedded images to render mathematical expressions from a fragment of an online journal article from *ACM Transactions on Mathematical Software* (the background of the article text has been shaded to show more clearly the location of the embedded images, all of which were captured with a white, non-transparent background). The embedded image approach allows rendering natively in the Web browser window, avoids client-side font issues, and is simple to implement on the server. HTML version 4 and CSS have reduced associated alignment difficulties and improved (from an appearance standpoint) the integration of the images.

Nonetheless this approach is still unsatisfactory in several ways. Embedded images of mathematical expressions are static, unlike the text that surrounds them. Changes in text font size and font family have no effect on the embedded math. Print resolution is limited to the resolution of the images (typically optimized for screen display and so of relatively low quality in print terms). The mathematics itself can't be searched directly and can't be captured except as a bitmapped image, making it useless as input for mathematical analysis tools such as Mathematica. Initial generation of the images and correct insertion of links into the HTML is cumbersome and demanding of resources, even when automated to maximum extent. Individual full-length journal articles may require the download of hundreds or even thousands of images, each download typically requiring the making and breaking of a separate connection between Webserver and Web browser. While equation image files are individually small, performance at both the server and client can be a problem due to sheer numbers of transactions, and bandwidth on a dialup line can become an issue. This approach of embedding mathematics in documents in the form of static images is primarily of use with documents containing only modest amounts of complex mathematics.

FIGURE 1. HTML Version of Article with Embedded PNG Images for Mathematics

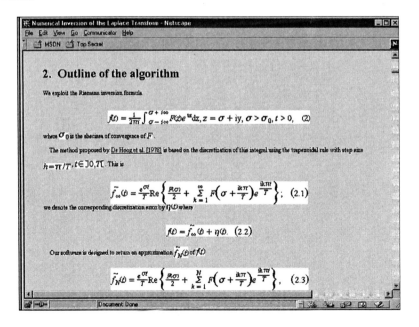

PAGE-ORIENTED MATHEMATICS FORMATS ON THE WEB

Most printed materials produced today are computer typeset using printed page-oriented digital formats such as T_EX and Adobe's Postscript (PS) and PDF formats. An approach to publishing mathematics on the Web is to make use of browser helper applications and plug-ins built to exploit the availability of these printed page-oriented digital versions of traditionally published works. As an alternative to embedding images of math equations in HTML, this approach better leverages the extensive work that has been done on developing high quality, printed page-oriented mathematical typesetting tools.

The success of this approach in any large-scale implementation depends on the universal (or near universal) availability and affordability of appropriate, high-quality helper applications and plug-ins. Adobe's Acrobat Reader for PDF, now available as a browser plug-in, is far and away the most ubiquitous of the available "viewer" plug-ins. It's also free. Not surprisingly then, PDF is the most commonly used printed page-oriented format on the Web today. Fortunately for those authoring and publishing documents containing complex mathematics, PDF representations of complex mathematics are generally quite good. PDF is a descendent of PS, itself a preeminent typesetting page description language still in widespread use among commercial and non-profit publishers. Figure 2 shows a fragment of an online journal article rendered as a PDF document.

PDF has several advantages as an interchange format for information on the Web. Required fonts are embedded in PDF files to ensure consistent rendering across platforms. Mathematical expressions are truly integrated with document text, e.g., changing size with surrounding text. Components of mathematical expressions can be selected and searched within a given PDF document. In recent years Acrobat has added many hypertext-like features and functions previously only found in Web browsers, and there are techniques authors can use to take maximum advantage of these features, especially for content only intended for the online environment (e.g., see Gossens and Rahtz 1999, pp. 59-61).

T_EX on the Web is another page-oriented format well suited for documents containing complex mathematics. For most research mathematicians writing today, T_EX is the preferred approach to authoring, so continuing to use it for Web publishing is a natural transition. In a Web environment T_EX files can be utilized directly, but more often T_EX output, in the form of DVI files, is used to avoid having to identify and transmit all the ancillary macro definitions and other components required

FIGURE 2. Article Viewed Using Adobe Acrobat Plug-In

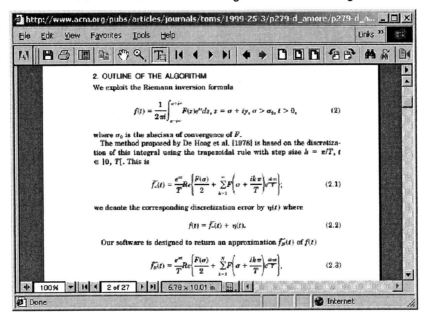

when using a T_EX file directly. Because Acrobat is so much more common on the desktop than DVI viewers (e.g., Personal T_EX's free DVI viewer, DVIScope), tools that transform DVI into PDF have also been developed so that authors can create using a T_EX authoring tool and disseminate using PDF. Like PDF, DVI can be used to encode entire documents and gives authors and publishers tight control over what the end-user sees on the screen. Unlike PDF, DVI files contain only the identity of the font sets required, not the font sets themselves.

PDF and DVI in a Web environment have limitations, however. PDF is still a proprietary format controlled by Adobe. Mathematical expressions in PDF and DVI documents are not interactive. Mathematical content copied from a PDF (or DVI) document is encoded in a way only PDF (or DVI) applications understand, meaning a user still can't paste mathematics into another, non-PDF (non-DVI) application (e.g., Mathematica) to any good effect. Both PDF and DVI remain page-oriented and presentation-oriented formats, retaining all the constructs of the printed page (e.g., fixed page breaks and line breaks) when migrated to the online environment. Content is essentially static and monolithic. Semantic meaning of the mathematics (and of other intellectual structures within the documents) is not well described, particularly not by PDF. As a result, cross document indexing and processing (e.g., the extraction of arbitrary metadata) is difficult and can only be done to a limited extent. Both PDF and DVI still require specialized software applications beyond the basic Web browser. These systems were developed for print publishing and retrofitted to the Web later. These formats are best used when migrating static documents (usually already in print or planned for print publication) to the Web, especially when the Web version of the document is considered ancillary or secondary to the print version.

LEGACY SGML ON THE WEB

Before there was HTML, there was SGML (Standard Generalized Markup Language). Like HTML, SGML was designed for documents created and intended for use in an online environment. Unlike HTML, SGML is a meta-language, defining the rules for describing markup language semantics and syntax specific to a particular community or function. HTML is a specific implementation or instance of SGML. Another SGML implementation, described in ISO Standard 12083:1994 ("Information and Documentation–Electronic Manuscript Preparation and Markup"), defines markup semantics and content models for representing article literature, book literature, and complex mathematics. Most SGML implementations intentionally decouple presentation of a document from its intellectual structure. Separate style sheets, optimized for a particular medium, are created to manage rendering of SGML files that describe the intellectual structure and content of a collection of documents. This means (given the right style sheets and rendering agents) that a single SGML file can be used to generate both a high quality printed page view of a document and an optimized online view. Many sci-tech journal publishers make use of SGML during the publishing cycle, sometimes alongside PS and/or PDF. Another approach to Web publishing of materials containing mathematics is to work from SGML representations of those materials.

Unfortunately, while several stand-alone SGML authoring and publishing tools can render mathematics with reasonably good fidelity, there are currently no SGML viewers available as Web browser plug-ins or helper applications that render mathematics in a satisfactory manner. With the advent of XML, most development work on improving SGML plug-ins and helper applications has stopped. (XML became a W3C Recommendation in 1998 and was intended to update the best features of SGML for greater compatibility with the Web environment.) On the plus side, SGML can readily (and quickly) be transformed into HTML (and XML). In the Illinois Testbed we have had limited success transforming legacy SGML into HTML (version 4) and using CSS (Levels 1 and 2) to render these legacy-derived HTML documents with a near acceptable measure of fidelity (Cole, Habing, and Mischo 2000). Figure 3 shows a fragment of an article transformed from SGML to HTML and rendered using CSS.

While the fidelity of this sample is not bad, neither is it good enough. Vertical spacing is difficult to control with any precision. Also, though not obvious from this sample, there are significant difficulties stretching fences and radicals, stacking multiple diacritics, and handling matrices and vectors. In addition, the investment of time to construct comprehensive style sheets for a large collection of documents containing a wide range of mathematical expressions and constructs is quite large. Completeness and sophistication of CSS implementations vary by Web browser brand and version, meaning that variant style sheets must be con-

FIGURE 3. Article Viewed in HTML 4 Using CSS to Render Mathematics

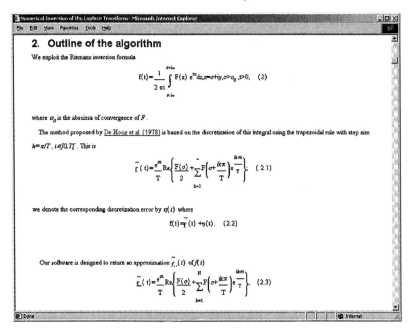

structed to deal with different browsers, and some browsers/browser versions simply can't be used to render the content at all. Finally, available SGML standards for markup of mathematics, though good, are not uniform, are incomplete, and their semantics tend to focus more on details of presentation than on meaning of math constructs described. Most publishers and SGML implementations designed to include complex mathematics have had to extend ISO 12083 semantics. The cost of developing canonical style sheets for the whole range of different SGML mathematics schemas in use would be prohibitive. For the Illinois Testbed we have decided instead to transform legacy SGML mathematics to presentational MathML for rendering using MathML-aware tools.

INTERACTIVE MATHEMATICS ON THE WEB

The limitations of HTML as a format for complex mathematics were recognized early on. Efforts to include advanced mathematical semantics in HTML version 3.2 were largely unsuccessful and led to the chartering in April 1997 of the W3C Mathematics Working Group. At about this same time proposals were being made for wholesale revisions in existing SGML schemas for mathematics (e.g., Buswell 1996), and work also was well along on the creation and development of the OpenMath architecture (Dewar 2000). An early conclusion of the W3C Mathematics Working Group (shared by the others mentioned) was that "to take full advantage of the interactivity offered by the Web, representations of mathematics not only should represent the appearance of the mathematical equations, but also should permit retention of the meaning of the equations as well" (Hagler 1998). The newest and arguably most interesting approaches to publication of mathematics on the Web share this premise.

The difference between "presentation" and "content" descriptions and markup of mathematics can be most easily understood by example. For instance, a superscript 2 may mean functional composition, e.g., f^2, or multiplication, e.g., x^2, or a second cohomology group, e.g., H^2 (from Carlisle 2000). When describing these expressions for printing on a page, all three of these constructs can be encoded the same way. The reader will deduce meaning from the context (i.e., the natural language text surrounding the expressions). There is no need for the computer typesetting system to distinguish among these different constructs since they will look equivalent on the page. A page-oriented presentational description language like T_EX, DVI, PS, or PDF is perfectly adequate for describing the printed view of these expressions. But if the mathematics is to be manipulated or analyzed by a computer algebra system (e.g., Mathematica, Maple, REDUCE), the subtle differences in meaning must be preserved and a more content-oriented, semantic markup scheme is required. "Computational systems lack the ability to use context to understand the semantics of a mathematical denotation. If we wish mathematics to be reliably communicated between such systems, we must mark up the document to provide extra semantic information" (Caprotti and Carlisle 1999).

To address the shortcomings of HTML for representation of mathematics and as a unifying step to bridge the gap between presentational and content-oriented schemes, the W3C Mathematics Working Group developed the MathML specification (current release is version 2, available at http://www.w3.org/TR/MathML2/). MathML, a specific community implementation of XML, includes semantics both for presentation and content markup of mathematics. Elements of both schemes can co-exist in a single document. Though some extensibility is provided, MathML is designed in particular to express mathematics as taught through first year of college level mathematics (Carlisle 2000). A second and complementary scheme, OpenMath (http://www.OpenMath.org), now also available as an XML implementation, is more exclusively a scheme for content markup of mathematics. By design MathML content semantics duplicate and overlap with OpenMath core semantics, but OpenMath goes further to support advanced mathematics and better facilitates extensibility (e.g., through OpenMath Content Dictionaries). The two approaches should be viewed more as complementary than competing.

While the definitions of MathML and OpenMath are detailed and well thought out, implementations for rendering documents containing MathML and OpenMath content are still in nascent stages. Most of the rendering implementations currently available (e.g., Mozilla, Amaya, IBM TechExplorer, Design Science WebEQ) focus on the rendering of presentation MathML markup. Fortunately, XML style sheet transformation (XSLT) templates are available for "dumbing-down" both content (semantic) MathML markup and OpenMath markup to presentational MathML markup (Carlisle 2000).

Figures 4 and 5 show an article fragment containing presentation MathML elements rendered natively by Mozilla (Figure 4) and rendered using the IBM TechExplorer ActiveX control (Figure 5). These examples illustrate the advantages of using MathML. Because MathML is an XML

FIGURE 4. Article Viewed Using Mozilla with MathML Support (Build 0.9.2)

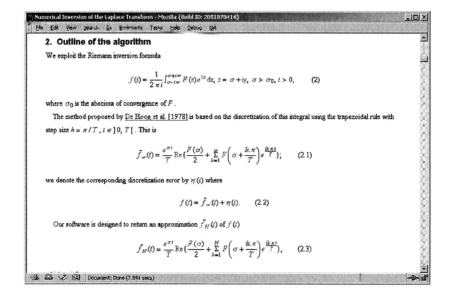

FIGURE 5. Article Viewed Using IBM TechExplorer ActiveX Control

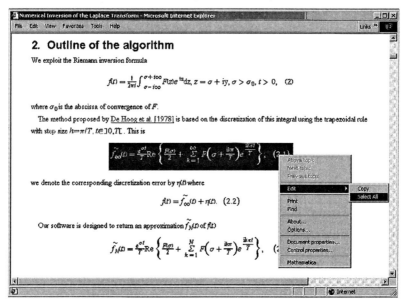

implementation, the potential exists to render MathML encoded mathematics natively in a Web browser window. This has been demonstrated by both the Mozilla browser (shown) and by the W3C's Amaya browser. (The mathematics community continues to lobby commercial Web browser vendors to add similar functionality, but so far to little effect.) While Microsoft's Internet Explorer (IE) currently does not support MathML natively, IE's support for third-party ActiveX controls allows much the same result. Being able to render MathML directly in the Web browser window allows authors to tightly integrate mathematics into their HTML or XML Web documents while preserving the ability to manipulate that mathematics and use it in whole or in part in local applications (e.g., computer algebra software). Figure 5 illustrates how an equation (or any part of an equation) can be copied to the clipboard by the IBM TechExplorer ActiveX control for use in other MathML-aware applications (i.e., latest versions of most computer algebra software). In this instance the TechExplorer application is able to exploit advanced "behaviors" of Microsoft Internet Explorer (IE) to seamlessly integrate its rendering of the mathematics with IE's rendering of surrounding text.

Figure 6 shows this integration taken to an even higher level. In this HTML page the embedded MathML is encoded such that the TechExplorer ActiveX control can send it to the Mathematica Kernel (running either locally or elsewhere on the Web) for evaluation. The Mathematica kernel then returns evaluation results to TechExplorer (as MathML) and TechExplorer then inserts these results into the browser window display. This simple illustration of interactivity is a foreshadowing of what can be anticipated, as more applications are developed to take advantage of MathML and OpenMath as interoperability solutions. Both client-side (e.g., Java Applets) and server-side (e.g., CGI and Servlets) interactive mathematics implementations built around MathML have been developed already, e.g., Project CATHODE (Wright 2000), the WebEQ Equation Input Control, and WebMathematica.

CONCLUSIONS

In summing up the current state of "Math on the Web," Robert Miner and Paul Topping of Design Science report that, "though there are many technologies available for Math on the Web projects, none of them is ideal. . . . The problem with current technologies for putting math on the Web is that they are too complicated and ad hoc . . . [and] no single approach provides a complete answer" (Miner and Topping 2001). Each of

FIGURE 6A. HTML Page Before User Clicks on Equations

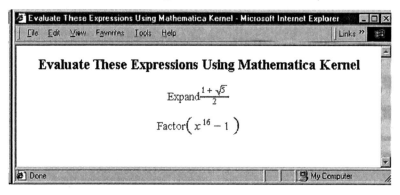

FIGURE 6B. HTML Page Updated by TechExplorer with Results from Mathematica

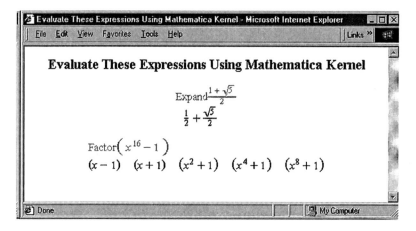

the techniques in widespread use today has advantages and disadvantages. Historically, Web technologies and the wide array of divergent technical approaches available in the Web environment, have been more of a hindrance than a help to authors and publishers of materials that include complex mathematical content. But lately the situation has become clearer.

PDF and DVI implementations tend to dominate today and have established their value for certain kinds of applications, but they have the very real drawback of being too static and printed page-oriented to fully exploit the potential of the Web as a dynamic and interactive medium. More dynamic approaches lag, but recent progress in the development and refinement of standards like MathML, OpenMath, and Unicode, more and better implementations of these standards in generally available applications, and a growing recognition by the community of the importance and value of dynamic and interactive mathematics on the Web are cause for optimism. In particular, recent implementations from IBM, Design Science, Wolfram, the Mozilla project, and the W3C demonstrate the potential of MathML as an adaptable, dynamic, and robust scheme for encoding and sharing mathematical content in the Web environment. Continued advances will enhance the usefulness of the Web, not only as a repository for digital versions of traditional printed materials containing complex mathematics, but also as a medium suitable for implementation of dynamic and interactive science and math information resources.

REFERENCES

Buswell, S., Healey, S., Pike, E. R., and Pike, M. S. (1996). "SGML and the Semantic Representation of Mathematics," presented at *DLI SGML Mathematics Workshop*, 1 May, Urbana, Illinois (unpublished).

Caprotti, O. and Carlisle, D. (1999). "OpenMath and MathML: Semantic Mark Up for Mathematics," *ACM Crossroads*, vol. 6 (2). Online. Available <http://www.acm.org/crossroads/xrds6-2/openmath.html> [25 July 2001].

Carlisle, David (2000). "OpenMath, MathML and XSL," *SIGSAM (Special Interest Group on Symbolic and Algebraic Manipulation) Bulletin*, vol. 34 (2): 6-11.

Cole, Timothy W., Mischo, William H., Habing, Thomas G., and Ferrer, Robert H. (2001). "Using XML & XSLT to Process and Render Online Journals," *Library Hi Tech*, vol. 19 (3): in press.

Cole, Timothy W., Habing, Thomas G., and Mischo, William H. (2000). "Illinois DLIB Testbed Technologies for Converting Legacy Mathematics for Display on the Web," presented at *MathML International Conference 2000: MathML and Math on the Web*, 21 October, Urbana, Illinois. Online. Available <http://www.mathmlconference.org/materials/Habing.zip> [25 July 2001].

Dewar M. (2000). "OpenMath: An Overview," *SIGSAM (Special Interest Group on Symbolic and Algebraic Manipulation) Bulletin*, vol. 34 (2): 2-5.

Goossens, Michel and Rahtz, Sebastian (1999). *The L^AT_EX Web Companion: Integrating T_EX, HTML, and XML*, Reading, Massachusetts: Addison-Wesley.

Hagler, Marion (1998). "Mathematics and equations on the WWW," *Proceedings of IEEE Computer Society Symposium Frontiers in Education: Moving from 'Teacher-Centered' to 'Learner-Centered' Education*, Piscataway, New Jersey: IEEE, vol. 2: 583-586.

Knuth, Donald E. (1979). "Mathematical Typography," *Bulletin (New Series) of the American Mathematical Society*, vol. 1 (2): 337-372.

Krantz, Steven G. (2001). *Handbook of Typography for the Mathematical Sciences*, New York: Chapman & Hall/CRC.

Miner, Robert and Topping, Paul (2001). *Math on the Web: A Status Report*, Long Beach, California: Design Science, Inc. Online. Available <http://www.dessci.com/webmath/status/status_Jan_01.stm> [25 July 2001].

Mischo, W.H. and Cole, T.W. (2000). "Processing and Access Issues for Full-Text Journals," in Harum, S. and Twidale, M. (Ed.), *Successes and Failures of the Digital Library Initiative, Proceedings of the 35th Annual Clinic on Library Applications of Data Processing*, Urbana, Illinois: Graduate School of Library and Information Science, University of Illinois at Urbana-Champaign, 21-40.

Schatz, B., Mischo, W.H., Cole, T.W., Bishop, A., Harum, S., Johnson, E., Neumann, L., and Chen, H. (1999), "Federated Search of Scientific Literature: A Retrospective on the Illinois Digital Library Project," *IEEE Computer*, vol. 32 (2): 51-60.

Wright, Francis J. (2000). "Interactive Mathematics via the Web Using MathML," *SIGSAM (Special Interest Group on Symbolic and Algebraic Manipulation) Bulletin*, vol. 34 (2): 49-57.

Creative Applications
of a Web-Based E-Resource Registry

Winnie S. Chan

SUMMARY. Electronic resources have become a staple feature of mainstream library access. Librarians are employing several methods to provide enhanced access to e-resources for end users and to make maintenance more efficient for staff. This paper shows how the e-resource registry approach can be integrated with existing custom Web-based services in order to extend their functionality to provide enhanced access to e-resources. The paper describes the e-journals relational database that describes resources licensed by the University of Illinois at Urbana-Champaign Library and illustrates its interactions with other Web applications developed at the Grainger Engineering Library. *[Article copies available for a fee from The Haworth Document Delivery Service: 1-800-HAWORTH. E-mail address: <getinfo@haworthpressinc.com> Website: <http://www.Haworth Press.com> © 2001 by The Haworth Press, Inc. All rights reserved.]*

KEYWORDS. E-resource registry, e-resource metadata, full-text journals, ASP applications, electronic journals database structure

Winnie S. Chan, MLS, is Assistant Engineering Librarian for Computer Services, University of Illinois at Urbana-Champaign, Urbana, IL.

The author wishes to acknowledge that John Weible, Acting Director of the UIUC Library Systems Office, provided the leadership in the creation of the e-resource registry at UIUC. He and his research programmer, Adam Lewenberg, provided the programming and management of the ready-made ASP Web applications described in this article.

[Haworth co-indexing entry note]: "Creative Applications of a Web-Based E-Resource Registry." Chan, Winnie S. Co-published simultaneously in *Science & Technology Libraries* (The Haworth Information Press, an imprint of The Haworth Press, Inc.) Vol. 20, No. 2/3, 2001, pp. 45-56; and: *Electronic Resources and Services in Sci-Tech Libraries* (ed: Mary C. Schlembach, and William H. Mischo) The Haworth Information Press, an imprint of The Haworth Press, Inc., 2001, pp. 45-56. Single or multiple copies of this article are available for a fee from The Haworth Document Delivery Service [1-800-HAWORTH, 9:00 a.m. - 5:00 p.m. (EST). E-mail address: getinfo@haworthpressinc.com].

45

INTRODUCTION

Electronic journals, once considered a rarity or even a privileged service only a few years ago, are a staple feature of mainstream library access that users have come to expect (Hurd 2001). The University of Illinois at Urbana-Champaign (UIUC) Library presently provides access to over 4,700 electronic journals for its users. To cope with today's information technology and the growth of the internet, libraries are employing several methods to provide enhanced access to electronic journals for end users and to make maintenance more efficient for staff. In their survey of academic library Web sites, Rich and Rabine identified a number of methods being used to provide access to electronic resources (Rich and Rabine 1999). There are two primary methods for providing electronic access to full-text journals: one through the online catalog, and the other through a custom e-resource database or registry. For various reasons many academic libraries have turned to e-resource registry as a more efficient and easier to maintain method for providing access to electronic journals (Lakos and Gray 2000, Jordan 2000). Also, some libraries are generating e-resource databases from online catalog data.

At the UIUC Library, access to full-text resources is accomplished through a centrally-maintained Web-based e-resource registry that allows individual departmental libraries and subject specialists to populate the database in order to produce custom Web lists of e-journals. This flexibility allows individual library units to generate subject-specific e-journals Web pages for their primary users. As Chrzastowski noted, this Web list model provides users the most convenient and *least effort* choice for accessing e-journals (Chrzastowski, 1999). The e-resource registry produced at UIUC is similar in structure and function to other e-resource registries created at other universities (Jordan 2000, Morgan 2000).

The e-resource registry structure consists of a set of dynamic server-side scripting Web applications, which utilize Object Database Connectivity (ODBC) protocols to provide dynamic access and updates to the contents of the e-journals relational database. A review of recent literature indicates a number of approaches for the organization of databases designed for managing library resources, many of which are from the developer point of view (Harker 1999, Gambles 2000, Cole et al. 2000, Port and Sponsler 2001). This paper will show how the e-resource registry approach can be integrated with existing custom Web-based services in order to extend their functionality to provide enhanced access to e-resources. In essence, this integration is accomplished by extracting various custom data from the e-resource registry depending on the applications needed.

ELECTRONIC RESOURCE PROFILE AND TEMPLATE

In late 1999 the UIUC Library charged an ad hoc Library Gateway committee to provide a strategic policy and recommendations for managing electronic resources and site licensing agreements for the UIUC Library as a whole. Prior to this time many of the 40 subject-specific departmental libraries maintained their own e-resource Web lists independently. Based on the guidelines and specifications recommended, the Library Systems programming staff created an electronic journals relational database for retrieval and display from departmental library homepages in addition to the Library Gateway Web page. The architecture and the contents of the database were continually enhanced in the following year to incorporate more functionality to meet current needs. The e-journals relational database is administered centrally by the staff of the Library Systems Office, and yet retains the necessary capability allowing the departmental units to enter, update or share data.

Each electronic resource is described according to a profile of metadata (see Table 1) and is given a unique record identifier (RID) automatically as the resource is being entered into the database. As such, the e-resource relational database truly serves as an "e-resource registry" for all UIUC licensed online journals. The database is accessible but password protected for maintenance purposes on the Main Library server. Staff members from departmental libraries use a Web form as template (Figure 1) to enter or edit the metadata of the e-resources that they have selected for their specific library and discipline.

Once a resource profile was created by one library, other subject-specific libraries can share the full-text link data from their e-journals Web page simply by adding their unit code to the "Unit Library Ownership(s)" field of the e-resource registry. However, the integrity of the resource metadata remains the responsibility of the library or librarian listed in the "Library Contact" field. Table 1 shows some of the essential profile data from the e-resource registry.

READY-MADE SCRIPT FILES

As mentioned earlier, prior to the adoption of this Web list model at UIUC, the departmental libraries designed their own subject-specific Web pages to provide users with links to full-text journals and other e-resources in their respective disciplines. The investment in maintaining these Web pages, however "flat" they are, required extensive staff time at each site, not to mention the duplicating efforts that staff at various sites might have spent on locating the same e-resource.

TABLE 1. Electronic Resource Metadata Profile Data

Resource Metadata Field	Options or Description
Access Type	• IP address • UIUC patrons • Limited • Global
Alternate Title(s)	
Availability Status	• Three options: Active; Trial; Delete
Created and Modified Dates	
Description of the Resource	
Universal Resource Location (URL)	• Including a proxy server anchor link
ISSN Online	
ISSN Print	
Language	
Library Contact	
Notes	
Publisher of the Print Version	
Record Identifer	• A non-repeatable, autonumber
Reported Date of Access Problem	
Subject(s)	• Selected from a list of preset terms
Title of the Resource	
Type of Resource	• A full-text journal
Unit Library Ownership(s)	• Linking the resource to the library's Web page
Usage Count	• A running total count of downloads at the article level
Vendor, Aggregator, or Resource Provider	• Selected from a list of preset names

At the beginning of the implementation of the e-resource registry, the Library Systems programming staff provided a set of dynamic server-side scripting Web applications in the form of Active Server Pages (ASP) files to perform various retrieval functions with the registry. For staff use, some of these script files perform maintenance activities, including searching for duplicating ISSNs (i.e., *issnduplist.asp*), adding new records (i.e., *search.asp* and *input.asp*, etc.), editing existing profile (i.e., *edit.asp*), and testing for unproxied sites. For public use, there are

FIGURE 1. Resource Profile Template Web Form

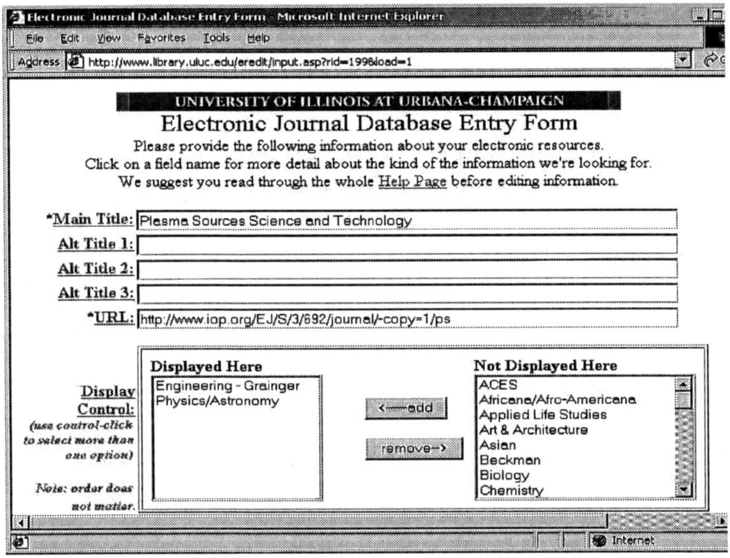

ready-made script files designed to generate Web lists (i.e., *all.asp* and *ejournals.asp*), a Web page about the resource (*details.asp*), and a link to get the URL via the RID number (i.e., *get.asp*). The "all UIUC" *all.asp* generates a list of all UIUC licensed e-resources while the "one-library" *ejournals.asp* lists those with ownership shown in the "Unit Library Ownership(s)" field of the registry. With the same formatting subroutines and functions embedded in the ASP script files, individual library Web lists are rendered in a standardized format displaying the type and status of e-resource access, online holdings and availability of the print version at UIUC. Such uniformity in appearance helps create consistency for end-users and staff members.

CREATIVE WEB APPLICATION
IN AN INTEGRATED ENVIRONMENT

Integrating with Web-Based Local Databases

The Grainger Engineering Library Information Center at UIUC has long been providing users and staff enhanced access to important information resources through a number of locally developed Web-based databases from the library's homepage (Mischo and Schlembach, 1999). With the implementation of the centrally-administered full text e-resource registry, it has been possible to enhance the local databases that contain currently received journals with information from the e-resource profile records. This is accomplished by linking the currently received journal information with the e-resource's RID from the registry. The unique RID is used with an ASP script file to connect to the URL of the specific journal.

The importance of the RID approach cannot be overestimated. Using the unique and persistent RID in lieu of the publisher's URL (which often changes) saves us from updating the invalid full-text links at various places within a number of local databases when a full-text URL changes. In other words, this approach allows us to store the journal's RID in a number of local databases and not be forced to change link data in the event that the URL changes.

For example, *Plasma Sources Science and Technology*, has a RID number, 199. Having the RID number in the notes field in the 'Currently Received Journals' database record for this journal allows a link to be placed in the Web page that displays the journal information to provide a connection to the online version. In this example, the URL below:

http://www.library.uiuc.edu/eresources/get.asp?rid=199

provides a link to the online version of the journal. From this now enhanced version of the currently received journals dynamic Web page, the user is given the current check-in information and the option of linking to the full-text version of the journal (Figure 2).

Since online version availability is displayed on the same Web page with print version availability, we have effectively increased the functionality of this locally developed database. From the same Web page users may also find links to the Table of Contents of a specific issue. The Table of Contents display is taken from the Institute for Scientific Information (ISI) Current Contents database. Figure 3 shows a Table of Contents display screen for *Plasma Sources Science & Technology*. As in our previous example, a reference to the online version via the resource's RID number, i.e., 199, is provided. It should be emphasized that these pages are generated dynamically using ASP technology and the RID stored in the local journals database is used in each of these pages to generate the full-text links.

FIGURE 2. Use of RID for a Currently Received Journals Search Result

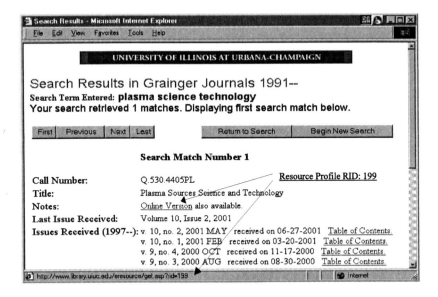

FIGURE 3. Use of RID from the Table of Contents Display Screen

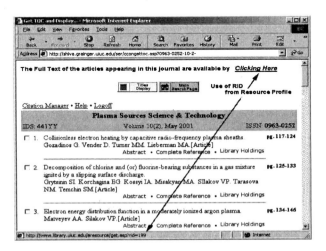

Providing Additional Access Points and Increased Functionality

As mentioned earlier, the ready-made script files used for accessing the e-resource registry were designed by professional programmers so that subject-specific library personnel may be spared the technical burden of maintaining their own online resource Web lists. The system allows the production of alphabetical listings arranged by the 40 subject departmental library codes. It also provides the capability of additional retrieval features using the e-resource profile records and custom ASP pages. Here are some examples to show how this functionality is used within the Grainger Engineering Library full-text e-journals homepage.

Within the ready-made script files, the database searching statements can be modified to perform Boolean searches on individual title words or to locate the online resource via an ISSN number. In this respect our custom Web list has become a search engine for the entire electronic resource collection (Figure 4).

While the standardized ASP script files are generating the custom Web lists dynamically from each subject-specific library's homepage, the basic coding of these ready-made Web applications may also be extended to

FIGURE 4. Use of "Title" and "ISSN" for Electronic Journal Searches

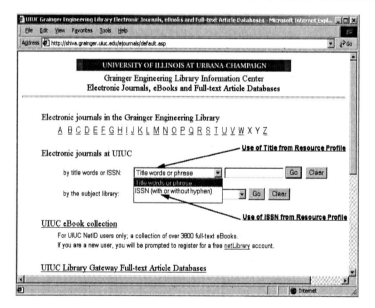

present a composite listing of libraries of common interest. We have provided access to individual libraries such as those within the Physical Sciences and Engineering Division and the Life Sciences Division libraries, so that users can navigate easily from one subject library to another without having to return to the Library Gateway to access another library's e-journals Web list (Figure 5).

It is not uncommon for users to utilize multiple subject-specific e-resource lists. This convenient listing of multiple libraries is very helpful in guiding both on-campus and remote users who may be accessing electronic journals from their homes, offices, laboratories or even off-campus. This is particularly useful to be able to switch among shorter but more relevant listings of full-text journals since it takes a long time to load the entire UIUC electronic journal collection and scrolling through the list is time-consuming.

Maintenance of Electronic Resources

One of the major problems with regard to e-journal licensing agreements is determining which titles are part of the subscription package. Many publishers include trial access to online journals for which the li-

FIGURE 5. Access to Other Library's E-Journal Lists

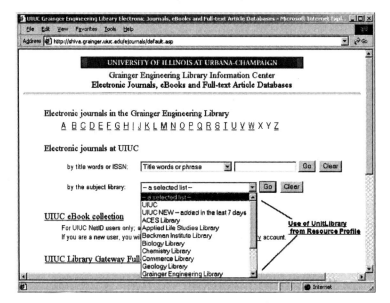

brary may not be subscribing in print. These titles are added into the e-re-source database, but they must be removed at the completion of the trial period. It is necessary to have a database structure that provides a mechanism to track titles by publisher, status and vendor information. The status field in the e-resource registry indicates (A) active subscription, (B) trial subscription, and (C) deleted title. For example, when the status is changed from B to C, titles available on trial basis are removed from the custom Web pages that are viewed by the public.

The publisher, status and vendor information fields can be used to produce custom lists on the Web for collection development librarians to examine. These lists can be generated by applying the "querying with querystring" technique that many search engines are using to pass data on to the server for data processing and posting. The querystring appended to a URL can even be processed by the server-side script of the requested Web page even without submitting a form. In our example in Figure 6, the report on demand is a list of Elsevier's ScienceDirect titles that Grainger Library has access to on a trial basis.

The querystring of the requested page (*erbyvenstatus.asp*), which is in the form of a leading question mark and three pairs of field names and their respective assigned field values, separated by ampersands, i.e.,

http://shiva.grainger.uiuc.edu/ejournals/erbyvenstatus.asp?group=enx&ven=27&stat=b

From this example report, librarians can keep abreast of the active subscriptions, trial subscriptions and deleted subscriptions within the ScienceDirect online service. At the end of trial period, some of the trial subscriptions may be assessed for purchase consideration. In that case, the status field will be changed to A. Or else the status of the expired e-resources will be changed to C.

CONCLUSION

The management of electronic resources can be time-consuming for librarians but nonetheless is necessary for maintaining effective full-text access. An e-resource registry approach to managing these online resources can be both efficient and effective. The examples in this paper demonstrate the use of metadata from a centrally-maintained e-resource registry with other locally developed Web applications. The persistent link data contained in the e-resource registry and custom script files are

FIGURE 6. Use of "Vendor" and "Status" for Tracking Online Trial Status

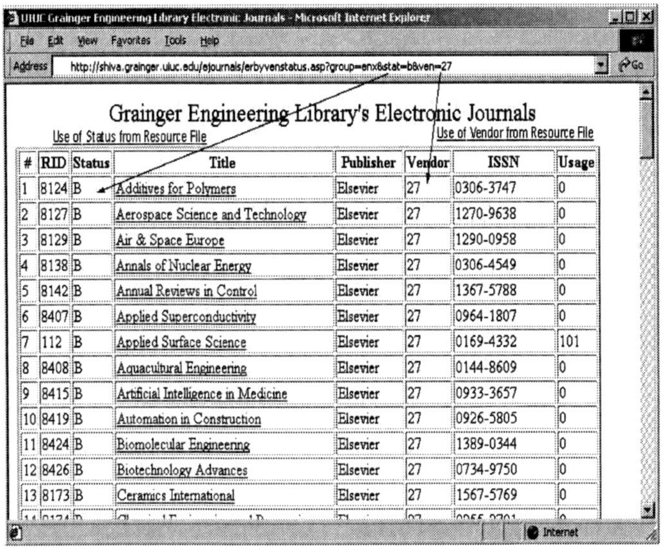

#	RID	Status	Title	Publisher	Vendor	ISSN	Usage
1	8124	B	Additives for Polymers	Elsevier	27	0306-3747	0
2	8127	B	Aerospace Science and Technology	Elsevier	27	1270-9638	0
3	8129	B	Air & Space Europe	Elsevier	27	1290-0958	0
4	8138	B	Annals of Nuclear Energy	Elsevier	27	0306-4549	0
5	8142	B	Annual Reviews in Control	Elsevier	27	1367-5788	0
6	8407	B	Applied Superconductivity	Elsevier	27	0964-1807	0
7	112	B	Applied Surface Science	Elsevier	27	0169-4332	101
8	8408	B	Aquacultural Engineering	Elsevier	27	0144-8609	0
9	8415	B	Artificial Intelligence in Medicine	Elsevier	27	0933-3657	0
10	8419	B	Automation in Construction	Elsevier	27	0926-5805	0
11	8424	B	Biomolecular Engineering	Elsevier	27	1389-0344	0
12	8426	B	Biotechnology Advances	Elsevier	27	0734-9750	0
13	8173	B	Ceramics International	Elsevier	27	1567-5769	0

being utilized in conjunction with Grainger Library local database applications. From the examples discussed in this paper, one can see how to enhance the Web functionality of a remote e-resource registry into an existing network environment with the use of persistent link data and by creating new database searching statements or custom querystrings data.

As a result, the Grainger Engineering Library not only shares its electronic resources through a centrally administered, e-resource registry, but also creatively provides enhanced access and custom reporting functions over the UIUC Library's online resources. The persistent link data approach can also be applied within the online catalog to minimize maintenance and prevent problems that occur with multiple or obsolete publisher URLs in the 856 fields of the cataloged record.

REFERENCES

Chrzastowski, T. E. 1999. E-journal access: the online catalog (856 field), Web lists, and the principle of least effort. *Library Computing* 18 (4):317-322.

Cole, Timothy W. and Robert S. Allen and John G. Schmitz. 2000. Building an Outreach Digital Library Collection. *Illinois Libraries* 82 (4):239-250.

Gambles, Anne. 2000. The development and launch of the HeadLine Personal Information Environment. *Information Technology & Libraries* 19 (4):199-208.

Harker, Karen R. 1999. Order out of chaos: Using a Web Database to Manage Access to Electronic Journals. *Library Computing* 18 (1):59-67.

Hurd, Julie M. 2001. Digital Collections: Acceptance and Use in a Research Community. *Crossing the Divide: Proceedings of the Tenth National Conference of the Association of College and Research Libraries*, ed. Hugh A. Thompson. Chicago: ACRL, 2001: 312-319.

Lakos, Amos and Chris Gray. 2000. Personalized Library Portals as an Organizational Culture Change Agent. *Information Technology and Libraries* 19 (4):169-174.

Mischo, William H. and Mary C. Schlembach. 1999. Web-Based Access to Locally Developed Databases. *Library Computing* 18 (1):51-58.

Morgan, Eric Lease. 2000. Guest Editorial: The Challenges of User-Centered, Customizable Interfaces to Library Resources. *Information Technology and Libraries* 19 (4):166-168.

Porter, George S. and Ed Sponsler. Online Journals: Utility of ToCs vs. Fulltext. *Crossing the Divide: Proceedings of the Tenth National Conference of the Association of College and Research Libraries*, ed. Hugh A. Thompson. Chicago: ACRL, 2001:110-119.

Rich, Linda A. and Julie L. Rabine. 1999. How libraries are providing access to electronic serials: A Survey of academic library web sites. *Serials Review* 25 (2):35-45.

Performance Measures
for Electronic Journals:
A User-Centered Approach

Julie M. Hurd
Deborah D. Blecic
Ann E. Robinson

SUMMARY. Libraries are spending increasing amounts to provide access to electronic journals. The decision to move toward digital collections is grounded in the belief that electronic journals offer significant benefits over their print counterparts. At present there is very little data to support that position because performance measures for electronic journals have not been fully developed. This paper describes a pilot study to test a methodology for evaluating electronic journals employing user-centered criteria. The study examined science and health sciences journal titles for which the library holds both paper and electronic subscriptions. *[Article copies available for a fee from The Haworth Document Delivery Service: 1-800-HAWORTH. E-mail address: <getinfo@haworthpressinc.com> Website: <http://www.HaworthPress.com> © 2001 by The Haworth Press, Inc. All rights reserved.]*

KEYWORDS. Evaluation of electronic journals

Julie M. Hurd, MA (Library Science), PhD (Chemistry), is Science Librarian, Coordinator of Digital Library Planning and Associate Professor; and Deborah D. Blecic, MLS, is Bibliographer for the Life and Health Sciences and Associate Professor, both at the University of Illinois at Chicago, Chicago, IL. Ann E. Robinson, MLIS, is Science Reference Librarian, Cabot Science Library, Harvard University, Cambridge, MA.

[Haworth co-indexing entry note]: "Performance Measures for Electronic Journals: A User-Centered Approach." Hurd, Julie M., Deborah D. Blecic, and Ann E. Robinson. Co-published simultaneously in *Science & Technology Libraries* (The Haworth Information Press, an imprint of The Haworth Press, Inc.) Vol. 20, No. 2/3, 2001, pp. 57-71; and: *Electronic Resources and Services in Sci-Tech Libraries* (ed: Mary C. Schlembach, and William H. Mischo) The Haworth Information Press, an imprint of The Haworth Press, Inc., 2001, pp. 57-71. Single or multiple copies of this article are available for a fee from The Haworth Document Delivery Service [1-800-HAWORTH, 9:00 a.m. - 5:00 p.m. (EST). E-mail address: getinfo@haworthpressinc.com].

57

INTRODUCTION

Library bibliographers and collection managers have developed numerous techniques to assess and evaluate print collections of monographs and journals. These tend to rely on librarians' subject expertise and understanding of the structure of the literature of various disciplines, as well as on their knowledge of users' needs and information seeking behavior. The professional literature includes many collection evaluation studies that support further acquisitions or provide input to serials cancellation projects. Now libraries are in the midst of transition as we move toward digital collections. In many disciplines databases have completely supplanted print indexes and abstracts; Index Medicus sits untouched on countless shelves while use of the PUBMED database continues to grow. Increasing numbers of scholarly journals are published in both print and electronic formats; some electronic journals exist that have no paper counterparts. A typical research library today numbers its electronic journal (hereafter, e-journal) subscriptions in the thousands. Most recently, electronic books have become part of our collections, and acquisitions funds are being spent on innovative Web-based products such as knowledge environments that have no parallels in print.

Approaches suitable for evaluating print collections may be only part of an assessment of digital collections. Of course, the content features still demand the bibliographers' subject expertise and knowledge of disciplinary literatures, but the technological aspects of an electronic resource add another dimension and additional complexity to any analysis. Content of an electronic resource is only one consideration; there are decisions made by the resource's developer that relate to hardware and software used to make that content accessible. The supporting technology, primarily hardware and operating system requirements, are of concern to library systems staff who will ensure that the necessary infrastructure is in place to allow use of the resource after it has been acquired by the library. Other technical features of the resource will be of greatest concern to users, and these will influence whether an expensive product is actually used by the intended market for it. These user-centered aspects of functionality include the retrieval system that was designed to support searching, the types of access to content that are supported, and the navigation permitted by the system interface. In this paper, we focus on performance measures for electronic journals that our interactions with library patrons suggest are important to them. User-centered criteria include content features such as currency and comprehensiveness as well as functionality aspects including linking and enhanced retrieval capabilities. Our analysis of e-journals will employ a framework provided by the Kano Model adapted from the Japanese management literature.

RELATED RESEARCH

As e-journals approach critical mass in many disciplines, librarians have asked questions about their timeliness and comprehensiveness. Several early studies of e-journal collections are comparative analyses of print versus Web-based versions of the same issues. Franck and Chambers (1998) examined twenty-six journals, primarily in the social sciences and humanities, represented in full-text collections provided by EBSCO, UMI, Information Access Company, and Wilson. The selected titles were also held in print by the SUNY Potsdam Library allowing the authors to collect issue-by-issue data on equivalency of content, availability of issues, and quality of graphics. They found substantial differences across publishers represented in their population and concluded that "full-text" has no standard definition in this context. Their study led them to conclude that the products they examined were not then ready to serve as complete substitutes for their paper counterparts. Shaffer and others (1999) at the Scripps Institution of Oceanography Library also compared timeliness of print versus electronic issues of journals to which the library subscribed in both formats. The authors collected and analyzed data on receipts over a six-week period to support collection development decisions. They reported that "84% of our print issues had electronic versions at the time of receipt, either the same issue number or future issue numbers."

Other evaluations of e-journals have focused on use statistics as performance measures, whether supplied by providers or generated locally. Mercer (2000) acknowledged the complexity and challenges in measuring use of digital resources. She described use statistics for HighWire Press and Ovid journals that provided not only a sense of the volume of use but also the breadth across disciplines and user groups. She recommended that librarians address measurement issues both locally and at higher levels to establish a set of minimal standards for basic use statistics. Morse and Clintworth (2000) compared use of a matched set of biomedical journal issues received in both print and Web-based formats at the Norris Medical Library, University of Southern California. They tracked print and electronic uses over a six month period monitoring 194 titles published during 1998. They found that the electronic versions were used over ten times as often as print and that usage patterns were remarkably similar for the print and electronic sets studied. Users' preference for electronic formats was also validated by Lenares (1999) who described findings from a 1999 survey of 500 faculty members at 20 universities whose libraries were members of the Association of Research Libraries. The author documented the growing acceptance of electronic journals by scholars in research institutions and interpreted her results using Everett Rogers' Diffusion of Information Theory (1995).

Electronic journals are clearly an emerging area of interest among librarians. The spring 2001 issue of the e-journal *Issues in Science and Technology Librarianship* (available at http://www.istl.org/) was devoted to articles that addressed "collection development in the Internet age." Two of the articles in that issue are particularly relevant to this study because they offer additional insights into evaluation of electronic journals. Faulkner and Hahn (2001) describe the development of a "genre statement"–a collection policy that assists in the evaluation and selection of electronic publications. Christie and Kristick (2001) outline an approach employed at Oregon State University to incorporate faculty input into a spreadsheet tool for setting priorities in building an e-journal collection. Both papers identify performance measures that reflect users' requirements and desires.

Evaluation of e-journals, whether to support pre-purchase decisions or post-purchase assessments, is complex and may involve cost-related and licensing considerations as well as user-centered measures. Criteria that reflect usability and value-added features for users include not only currency of electronic issues and comprehensiveness of content, when compared to print, but also functionality of the interface. Efforts to measure use by analysis of vendor- and institution-generated statistics seem likely to lead to efforts to standardize usage data so that cross-title and cross-provider comparisons can be meaningful. The Association of Research Libraries has recognized the importance of developing new measures for digital collections and has sponsored an "e-metrics" project to develop "a set of tools, processes, and techniques [that] will be useful to the library community in general as it looks to provide electronic resources to their communities." (See <http://www.arl.org/stats/program/newmeas.html> and <http://www.arl. org/stats/program/newmeas/emetrics/index.html>.)

THE KANO MODEL

The Kano model defines three levels of customer expectations–expected, normal, and exciting–that must be present for a product or service to succeed in the marketplace. Von Dran and Zhang (2000) developed a theoretical framework for assessing the quality of customer-centered Web sites that employed Kano's quality dimensions for products and services (ReVelle et al., 1998). They applied Kano's principles to the Web environment by viewing users as "customers" or "consumers" of the services provided by the Websites that they visit. Because human-to-human interaction is not a feature of Web-based activities, interface design is a critical element in service delivery. Von Dran and Zhang collected empirical data on features used in Website design and then applied Kano's framework to categorize their quality nature. Their approach demonstrated promise for the method and suggested additional areas of exploration. In this paper we test the applicability of the model to evaluation of electronic journals.

Figure 1 depicts the Kano model with its three levels of customer expectations and their relationship to user satisfaction. *Basic* (or expected) needs are the minimum attributes required by the marketplace. Those features for which "it goes without saying" make up this category. Only if a product fails to meet basic needs will the customer take note, and express dissatisfaction. For an e-journal the lack of full-text for the articles might fall into this category–it isn't an *e-journal* without substantive content. That the content can be accessed with a Web browser, with standard additional helper applications, such as Acrobat Reader, is another expected need, as is capability to provide a print, and possibly a downloadable copy of an article. Users will certainly complain if this level of functionality is lacking in an e-journal. Users also assume that an electronic version of an article will be available concurrent with its print appearance; failure to meet this expectation has generated more complaints than any other feature the authors have encountered.

Performance quality (or normal, expressed needs) includes those features that a typical user would articulate as desirable. They are the features that are uppermost in the mind of a user when making a decision to use a resource. A thoughtful user would automatically look for and evaluate these features. In an e-journal these might include:

- Thumbnails for tables and graphics that link to a page suitable for printing
- Text links to references in a bibliography
- Easy navigation among the sections of an article
- An interface that easily supports the traditional modes of journal use: browsing, known item, and author/subject searching.

FIGURE 1. The Kano Model

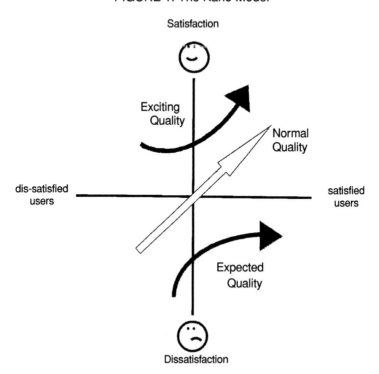

Exciting quality refers to innovative features that a user might not think to request but that would be warmly received, if available. Innovative features inspire loyalty and encourage repeated use. These make a product a market leader and speed adoption by its users. E-journals are just beginning to explore this area. Exciting features might include:

- Links to other journal articles cited
- Links to electronic pre-prints for "in press" articles
- Links to Chemical Abstracts or MEDLINE abstracts for articles cited
- Links to data repositories such as GenBank or other supplementary information
- Links to more information on a topic, e.g., encyclopedia articles or similar sources.

Science Online is an e-journal that displays numerous features that offer much more than a digitized version of the print product.

METHODOLOGY

The University of Illinois at Chicago (UIC) subscribes to over 3,000 electronic journals that are acquired through a variety of providers. Most of the electronic titles have print equivalents which are also received by the library. The authors of this study chose to focus on that subset of the e-journal collection that serves the basic sciences, technology, and the health sciences. Because our goal was to pilot an evaluative methodology, we chose a purposive sample that represented the diversity of the e-journal collection with respect to:

- All in-scope disciplines, broadly defined
- All major aggregators used by UIC
- Publisher collections, both profit-sector and society
- Major titles subscribed to on an individual basis.

We examined two issues of each title chosen for inclusion in our study and constructed a grid to record data collected for each title. Since the goal of this project was to pilot a method for evaluation, no statistics were generated. Averages would make no sense for the sample studied, but the range of a variable observed and an assessment of whether the measure is meaningful will be noted.

Table 1 lists the providers and titles that comprised our study population. We chose several titles because, at the time of data collection, we had access to them through more than one provider. Early on we were aware of differences in content and functionality among providers, and we wanted to explore whether our methodology might also have potential for evaluating aggregators.

MEASUREMENT OF USER-CENTERED CRITERIA

The appearance of a print issue of a selected title triggered data-gathering for that issue. Since the titles included in the study were either Science Library or Library of the Health Sciences journals, monitoring the new journal receipts was easily done. For each issue the following data were recorded:

Currency

When a print issue was received at its destination library, the Web edition was searched for the corresponding e-issue. We also noted whether there was an even more recent electronic issue on the site as well any "e-prints" for future issues (articles accepted for publication but not necessarily yet associated with a specific issue).

TABLE 1. E-Journal Providers and Titles Studied

Profit Sector Providers
Academic IDEAL
• Biochemical & Biophysical Research Communications
• Icarus
• Journal of Sound and Vibration
Elsevier ScienceDirect
• AIChE Journal
• Applied Catalysis A
• Fertility & Sterility
• Journal of Electron Spectroscopy & Related Phenomena
• Journal of Inorganic Biochemistry
• Thin Solid Films
Karger
• Human Heredity
MDConsult
• American Heart Journal
• Pediatrics
OCLC Electronic Collections Online (ECO)
• Biochemical & Biophysical Research Communications
• Geophysical Journal International
• Plant Molecular Biology
Ovid
• AACN Clinical Issues
• Fertility & Sterility
• New England Journal of Medicine
• Pediatrics

Society Publishers
American Association for the Advancement of Science (AAAS)
• Science Online
American Chemical Society (ACS)
• Journal of Agricultural & Food Chemistry
American Institute of Physics (AIP)
• Journal of Chemical Physics
Institute of Physics (IOP)
• Journal of Physics. Condensed Matter
Massachusetts Medical Society
• New England Journal of Medicine
National Academy of Sciences
• Proceedings of the National Academy of Sciences
Society for Industrial and Applied Mathematics (SIAM)
• Theory of Probability & Its Applications
• SIAM Journal on Applied Mathematics

Other
HighWire Press
• Journal of Biological Chemistry
SPARC (with ACS)
• Organic Letters

Comprehensiveness

With the print issue in hand, the electronic issue was checked for presence of all the content types present in print:

- Research articles
- Letters to the editor
- Communications
- Errata
- Classified advertising
- Display advertising
- News
- Columns

Not all the journals had all the various types of content listed above. This measure was intended to capture whether content was equivalent. In one case, we found articles in the digital version that were not provided to print subscribers.

Presence of Links

The electronic issue was examined for the presence of hotlinks to:

- Author Web pages or e-mail addresses
- Other full-text articles
- Databases such as EMBASE, MEDLINE, etc.
- Data repositories (GENBANK, ACS supplementary information, etc.)

Access to Journal Content

Each provider of electronic journals controls access to their content through the design of their interface. We looked for navigational features and search engine capability that supported browsing of individual issues, searching for a cited item for which volume, issue, and page were known, and searching for articles by a particular author or on a subject of interest.

Full-Text Options

We recorded the options offered users for full-text articles. Were there html versions with all the navigation that format permits? Were there PDF files suitable for making print copies? What helper applications were needed to access all the content of an article? For example, did readers need RealPlayer for audio clips?

System Documentation

Does a provider offer context sensitive documentation for users? Is there a "help" button or indexed documentation readily visible? Are there FAQ's for the providers' journals?

Personalization

Does the site offer users who register personalization options such as e-mailed notices of new issues, saved searches, or site customization?

CLICK COUNT: A MEASURE OF FUNCTIONALITY

Interactions with library users revealed the importance they placed on ease of navigation to reach a desired destination on a Web site. Whether it was simple expediency or use (typically from home) of a slow Internet connection, users wished to minimize mouse clicks. To capture that measure of functionality for e-journals, we propose a measure we will call the "click count." The *click count* is defined as the number of mouse clicks required to reach a desired Web page; the count begins after the user has selected a specific journal title from the library's Web listing of its electronic journals. Click counts may vary for the main types of searching done in a journal:

- Browsing latest issue
- Searching for a known article
- Searching by author or subject.

Some aggregators do not support a direct link to the journal page but require users to navigate through a gateway. For some journals, the author/subject search screen is linked from the gateway page; limiting to a specific title may be easily done, or not. Not all providers offer the three types of searching; that in itself is an important factor in an evaluation of a product.

For all journals included in this study the click count was determined for each of the types of searching offered by the journal provider. The count was measured by two investigators in an effort to identify accurately the minimum click count for each type of search. In some cases, depending on the efficiency of the route the tester selected, click counts could vary. The range of values measured is displayed in Table 2. Two sets of values represent data collected during spring 2000 and spring 2001 and reflect several interface redesigns that occurred during the year.

E-JOURNAL PERFORMANCE MEASURES

The user-centered criteria that were examined for each e-journal studied represented the authors' efforts to identify a set of meaningful performance measures. Mapping each of these to a Kano category of quality offers a framework in which to assess the relative importance of a particular measure.

TABLE 2. Click Count Range for Electronic Journals

Type of Search	Measured Spring 2000	Measured Spring 2001
Browse latest issue	1-8	1-4
Reach known item	3-8	2-6
Conduct author/subject search	2-7	2-5

We labeled as "basic needs" access to *full-text* of articles with a standard Web browser, the availability of *html* and *PDF* formats, and *currency* of issues as compared to print. Failure of an e-journal provider to satisfy these expected needs resulted in user dissatisfaction. The single aspect of e-journals that generated the most frequent user complaints was failure to provide an issue simultaneous with print or sooner. Research scientists are authors and now submit manuscripts to publishers in electronic format for most major journals. Correctly or not, they believe that this should speed the time to availability of content, and that electronic content should be ready for use prior to printing and mailing of the hardcopy issue. We would hear from users who were unable to access an electronic issue at the time that popular news media would feature a story from that issue. This was especially problematic with one of our primary providers. That provider had, early on, made a decision to provide only marked-up versions of full-text. This resulted in delays of several months before an issue would appear as most journals do not require SGML submissions from authors. That provider has recently moved to PDF versions as well and has tried to reduce any time lags in provision of content. For all providers studied, currency ranged from 1-3 electronic issues ahead of print to 2 issues behind.

Another case of failure to satisfy a basic need was the infrequent case of a provider who employed a definition of "full-text" unacceptable to readers. Users do not consider an abstract or an outline a satisfactory substitute for the full research article. However, for most of the issues examined, providers supplied all research articles that appeared in the print version. One publisher even offered additional articles in the online version of the journal that did not appear in print.

Performance level expectations were generally well-satisfied in the titles we examined. Most providers have developed quality Web-based publications that are *easy to read and navigate. Tables and graphics* display well, with an occasional difficulty in printing. An emerging concern may be the increasing use of color in journals, for example, complex chemical structures where color conveys information on molecular structure. Users with low-end, black-and-white only print capability will find printing frustrating and will lose information if they choose to print images rather than view them on-screen. Most providers offer all *basic searching capabilities*; the click counts quantify the ease of navigation within a resource. That the range of *click counts* has diminished over a year suggests that interface designers realize that users want to move quickly to desired full-text. Sometimes, enhancements must be implemented by the subscribing library to improve performance and minimize the click count. For example, the "jumpstart" feature for Ovid customers takes users directly to a particular journal and eliminates the need for users to go through gateway pages, but requires Web page coding by library staff.

We observed some variation in *subject searching* capability. One provider does not support full-text searching but uses only the bibliographic (source) information to support retrieval. On the other hand, users who employ a full-text search across a multidisciplinary collection of journals may experience large and very imprecise result sets. Advanced searching capabilities are not present in all e-journals; some support only simple search strategies that, for inappropriately-chosen search terms, may lead to many false drops. Examples of suitable search terms and context-sensitive help can address some of these shortcomings.

Personalization options are present in many products. Users typically are required to establish a personal account and subsequently use an ID and password to gain access to all the custom features available. Depending on provider, these options may include establishing a personal portal page that displays only journals of interest, setting up e-mail notification when new issues of a favorite title are available, arranging for automatic e-mailing of tables of contents, and saved searches.

"Exciting" quality features are an aspect of electronic journals evolving rapidly. Many providers are starting to think "outside the box" and are developing features that go beyond the print format's capabilities. Within the past year some interfaces have been completely redesigned; others are continually being upgraded with new features directed toward users. Exploiting the *linking* possibilities of the Web environment can make it possible for users to navigate easily among articles, references, non-textual material and more. The emergence of Cross-Ref and Link-Out in PUBMED are two examples of approaches to supporting increasing connectivity of information. Most users don't anticipate such features, but once they discover them they are extremely pleased. Another area where change is evident is in the access to numerous types of *non-textual information*, some even interactive, such as: molecular structures that can be rotated, genetic sequences, computer source code, mathematical models that can be manipulated, video and audio materials, and still more. Authors who free themselves from the limitations of the printed page will see opportunities to incorporate such features in their writing. Both linking and incorporation of non-textual information will necessarily cause print and electronic issues to diverge in content and functionality.

The Kano Model assumes that, over time, qualities will migrate across the three categories. Features once considered exciting will become normal expectations of users; normal quality features will be expected without saying. Figure 2 offers a checklist of performance measures for electronic journals grouped by Kano quality categories. Because e-journals are in an active developmental stage, we expect to see new qualities appear and existing measures shift among categories as users' experiences and expectations increase. Even during the past year interfaces have undergone redesign and providers' practices have changed; more change is to be expected with respect to both content and functionality of e-journals.

RECOMMENDATIONS

The price of an electronic journal, as well as licensing issues, often determines whether a library can consider acquisition. If cost and license are favorable, we recommend that further evaluation consider the users for whom the resource is intended, especially if there is more than one way to acquire an e-journal. Selectors should "test drive" the product and consider the features listed in Figure 2. The cheapest way to acquire an e-journal may not provide the best service to users. Compare titles across aggregators when possible; access and searching capabilities may vary dramatically. Set aside your fund-manager's green eyeshade and put on the scientist's lab coat. Use e-journals as the scientists will. Don't negotiate the license and arrange for payment without inspecting the product in-depth.

In addition, try to influence the direction of change by providing feedback to vendors on interface functionality, currency of issues, content, and more. Talk with scientists who serve on association and journal boards and advisory committees. Electronic journals represent our future. Let's do all we can to make them as functional as possible for scientists.

FIGURE 2. Checklist for E-Journals

Expected (Basic) Features

- fulltext
- Web browser access
- printing and downloading
- availability concurrent with print

Normal (Performance) Features

- availability prior to print
- quality tables and graphics displays, with printing
- easy navigation
- full range of searching and browsability
    - latest issue
    - known item
    - author/subject searching
- low "click count"

Innovative (Exciting) Features

- links, links, links . . .
    - to other articles
    - to abstracts
    - to data repositories
    - to supplementary information
- audio or video content

DIRECTIONS FOR FURTHER RESEARCH

Two of the authors of this paper are engaged, with colleagues, in an investigation of university faculty use of electronic journals. Faculty in the basic and health sciences are being interviewed to discover how electronic journals and other Web-based resources are changing the way they teach and do research. Those findings will be reported in subsequent presentations and publications.

REFERENCES

Christie, Anne and Kristick, Laurel. "Developing an Online Science Journal Collection: A Quick Tool for Assigning Priorities" *Issues in Science and Technology Librarianship* Spring 2001. Available at <http://www.library.ucsb.edu/istl/01-spring/article2.html>.
Faulkner, Lila A. and Hahn, Karla L. "Selecting Electronic Publications: The Development of a Genre Statement" *Issues in Science and Technology Librarianship* Spring 2001. Available at <http://www.library.ucsb.edu/istl/01-spring/article1.html>.

Franck, Carol and Chambers, Holly. "How Full Is the Full in Full-Text?" Poster session presented at the ALA annual conference, Washington, DC, June, 1998. Available at <http://www2.potsdam.edu/LIBR/franckcr/ALA.html>.

Lenares, Deborah. "Faculty Use of Electronic Journals at Research Institutions" *Association of College and Research Libraries 9th National Conference*, Detroit, MI, April 1999. pp. 329-334.

Mercer, Linda S. "Measuring the Use and Value of Electronic Journals and Books" *ISTL (Issues in Science and Technology Librarianship)*, Winter 2000. Available at <http://www.library.ucsb.edu/istl/00-winter/article1.html>.

Morse, David H. and Clintworth, William A. "Comparing Patterns of Print and Electronic Journal Use in an Academic Health Science Library" *ISTL (Issues in Science and Technology Librarianship)*, Fall 2000. Available at <http://www.library.ucsb.edu/istl/00-fall/refereed.html>.

Revelle, Jack B., Moran, John W. and Cox, Charles A. *The QFD Handbook*. New York: John Wiley & Sons, 1998. 410 pp. plus disk. See Appendix D, pages 359-365.

Rogers, Everett M. Diffusion of Innovations. Fourth Edition. New York: The Free Press, 1995.

Shaffer, Shelley, Berteaux, Susan S., Oswald, Brandon, and Breuggeman, Peter. "Going Electronic? Receipt of Print Journal Issues and Their Electronic Availability" *Proceedings of the 25th International Association of Aquatic and Marine Science Libraries and Information Centers Annual Conference*, Woods Hole, MA, October 1999. *In press.*

Von Dran, Gisela and Zhang, Ping. "A Model for Assessing the Quality of Websites" *Proceedings of the 63rd Annual Meeting of the American Society for Information Science*, v. 37: pp. 326-333, 2000.

A Brief History of E-Prints
and the Opportunities
They Open for Science Librarians

Kenneth L. Carriveau, Jr.

SUMMARY. Spiraling journal costs have plagued libraries for years and the Association of Research Libraries' 1994 investigation into pricing issues clearly illustrated the science librarian's predicament. This paper reviews how some scientists, as both producers and consumers of the information distributed through these journals, use electronic self-archives called e-prints to break the stranglehold journal publishers have over science libraries, and the opportunities open to librarians to facilitate and support the reformation. *[Article copies available for a fee from The Haworth Document Delivery Service: 1-800-HAWORTH. E-mail address: <getinfo@haworthpressinc.com> Website: <http://www.HaworthPress.com> © 2001 by The Haworth Press, Inc. All rights reserved.]*

KEYWORDS. E-prints, electronic publishing, scientific communication

INTRODUCTION

Science librarianship has changed significantly since computers were introduced to the profession in the 1960s, but never more so since the late

Kenneth L. Carriveau, Jr., BS (Chemical Engineering), MSLS, is Assistant Professor and Science/Engineering Reference Librarian, Baylor University, Waco, TX.

The author acknowledges the support and encouragement of William B. Hair and Olga Paradis, and thanks Phillip J. Jones for proofreading.

[Haworth co-indexing entry note]: "A Brief History of E-Prints and the Opportunities They Open for Science Librarians." Carriveau, Kenneth L., Jr. Co-published simultaneously in *Science & Technology Libraries* (The Haworth Information Press, an imprint of The Haworth Press, Inc.) Vol. 20, No. 2/3, 2001, pp. 73-82; and: *Electronic Resources and Services in Sci-Tech Libraries* (ed: Mary C. Schlembach, and William H. Mischo) The Haworth Information Press, an imprint of The Haworth Press, Inc., 2001, pp. 73-82. Single or multiple copies of this article are available for a fee from The Haworth Document Delivery Service [1-800-HAWORTH, 9:00 a.m. - 5:00 p.m. (EST). E-mail address: getinfo@haworthpressinc.com].

1980s and early 1990s when digital information resources were developed to take advantage of computer networks, especially the Internet, and of desktop multimedia capabilities. One area in which information technologies are creating a paradigmatic shift for science librarianship is the use of electronic archives to disseminate research findings among scientists instead of, or in addition to, the traditional print journals. This electronic alternative opens a number of opportunities for the science librarian, especially during these times of tight budgets and high service expectations from patrons.

SCHOLARLY COMMUNICATION AND JOURNALS: A BRIEF HISTORY

Until the mid-17th century, scholarly scientific discourse was limited to three basic venues: letters of correspondence among peers, personal meetings, or the occasional oral presentation at meetings of learned societies. Though they did protect the researcher from operating in isolation, their outreach capabilities, in terms of speed and geographic scope of distribution, were woefully inadequate to reach more than a few scholars within a particular discipline. As a result, replication of effort and data redundancy were common, and authorship for groundbreaking discoveries was sometimes unclear (Fjällbrant 1997).

During the 1600s learned societies and other organizations recognized these deficiencies of scholarly communication and sought to rectify the problem by introducing the "journal." The journal encapsulated the most recent news and research findings into a single document for large-scale dissemination. Years later, publishers introduced the peer review system that ensured researchers that the information presented within a journal was of high quality (Fjällbrant 1997). Over the years, the journal flourished and grew in prestige and importance within the scholarly community to the point that a scientist who wished to share information had to publish it in a journal in order for it to be recognized by peers. Of course the researcher still held the prerogative of distributing copies of the manuscript to whomever he wished but no longer could expect anyone, except perhaps his closest colleagues, to accept the work without question. In short, the journal usurped the researcher's ability to distribute findings directly to peers on a wide-scale. Also, since the journal was not free and its distribution was limited to those who could afford to pay its subscription price, the journal usurped the scientist's ability to hear about and discuss the research of colleagues at minimal cost. Technological limitations ensured that this restrictive situation endured until the late 20th century.

BIRTH OF THE E-PRINT

In the early 1990s, Stevan Harnad, a cognitive scientist then at Princeton, and Paul Ginsparg, a physicist at Los Alamos National Laboratory (LANL), recognized that recent advances in desktop computing and global telecommunications gave research scientists the opportunity to reconsider the necessity of using intermediaries to reach their colleagues. Unlike their predecessors, who envisioned using technology to improve existing systems of information delivery, Harnad and Ginsparg suggested that authors and research institutes establish electronic or "e-print" archives to challenge the journal industry's control over scholarly communication.

Harnad asserted that publishing an article is merely a step in the scientific communication process and focusing on that one point for technological applications is shortsighted. He coined the term "scholarly skywriting" to illustrate how information technologies are applied at all stages in the creative process from the origination of an idea, through refinement and informal peer review of draft manuscripts, until the final accepted copy of the manuscript is published (Harnad 1990). He refined this argument further in 1994 in an online forum on the future of scholarly journals when he presented and defended a "subversive proposal" on "ESOTERIC (non-trade, no-market) scientific and scholarly publication" (Okerson and O'Donnell 1995).

This "subversive proposal" seeks to use information technology to transform the process of scientific communication from one publisher dominated to one in which the researcher, as both producer and consumer of the information distributed in this process, controls the system. He asserts that, although technological limitations prevented them from being satisfied completely without the intervention of journals, the following conditions have always existed in the research community: (1) researchers want to share their findings with peers in order to gain recognition for their efforts rather than expecting to profit materially from it; (2) authors wish to distribute their results freely, widely, and quickly; (3) researchers wish to learn what their colleagues are doing in a timely and inexpensive manner; and (4) authors desire the freedom to use or replicate their own work whenever they want. Harnad claims that publishers have long taken advantage of these technological limitations and have profited handsomely by this effective monopoly (Okerson and O'Donnell 1995). With advances in desktop computing capabilities and telecommunications networks, it is now possible for open e-print archives to make research results available to anyone around the world with Internet access.

Researchers are now able to communicate quickly via electronic pathways with infinite numbers of colleagues at virtually no cost to the readers, and authors may choose to bypass journals when disseminating their information. Therefore, instead of wielding tremendous, authoritative power over which papers and theories are distributed, publishers should assume more supportive roles in scholarly discourse and limit their responsibilities to (1) ensuring that quality control via peer review continues to exist in the e-print system and (2) working with libraries to establish stable archival files of these scientific papers (Okerson and O'Donnell 1995).

While Harnad addressed the social and theoretical aspects of e-print archives, Paul Ginsparg took advantage of the strong preprint culture in theoretical high-energy physics (HEP-Th) and the computing prowess of LANL to create *xxx.lanl*, which is now called *arXive* <http://arXive.org>, the first Internet-based e-print server (Ginsparg 1994). Paper preprints have been crucial to scholarly communications in physics and astronomy for decades (Youngen 1998, Till 2001) and, initially, *arXive* was little more than the digital equivalent of paper preprint bibliographic tracking systems established at major research institutes like the Stanford Linear Accelerator (Parker 1971) and the National Radio Astronomy Observatory Library (Bouton and Stevens-Rayburn 1995). E-mail was the primary means of interacting with the server, and researchers learned about the database's existence through personal conversations with colleagues. Therefore, *arXive* was an improvement over the preprint mail and FAX delivery systems implemented in the 1960s and 1970s but did not reach the extent of Harnad's vision. In a few short years, however, as the Internet grew in sophistication and users became more adept at computing applications, *arXive* grew from its humble beginnings, with one subject discipline supported and a small number of subscribers, to an extensive database with multiple disciplines accessed by tens of thousands of users per week. Thus, by 1993, particle physicists and their colleagues were able to enjoy the free and open exchange of information encapsulated in Harnad's "scholarly skywriting" (Taubes 1993).

Buoyed by *arXive's* successful proof that electronic self-archives could deliver cutting-edge research faster than and as effectively as journals, numerous e-print servers began appearing around the world. For example, several foreign organizations established *arXive* mirror sites in their countries, the European Organization for Nuclear Research created the *CERN Preprint Library* <http://library.cern.ch/> (Dallman, Draper and Schwarz 1994), Harnad started the *CogPrints* archive <http://cogprints. soton.ac.uk/> at the University of Southampton to facilitate communication in the cognitive and related brain sciences (Taubes 1996a), and over fifty international institutions cooperated to create the *Networked Computer Science Technical Research Library* <http://www.ncstrl.org/> as a repository for their institutional publications on computer and information technology (Davis and Lagoze 2000). These successes and the dizzying pace of computing and telecommunication technologies development heralded the end of traditional journal publishing in the sciences (Odlyzko 1995).

DEATH OF THE JOURNAL?

But the grand revolution has not happened yet. Even though Ginsparg and others demonstrated that the technical limitations of electronic publishing were eliminated, several significant sociopolitical issues associated with publishing and scholarly discourse prevented the demise of scientific journals. Almost every group with an interest in scholarly scientific communication had representatives opposed to a complete change over to e-print archiving. Journal publishers were concerned about the threats that author self-archiving posed toward their financial growth and the loss of prestige their journals would experience within the research community if they were no longer the first to announce groundbreaking discoveries. Many publishers and editors viewed e-prints to be such serious threats to their industry that they modified their submission policies to exclude any manuscript previously or concurrently released on an e-print server from consideration for publication in their journal. Surprisingly, researchers, who would profit most from a change to the e-print system, also had their detractors. They were worried that electronic archiving would lead to an explosion of junk science, an increase in plagiarism, and the loss of recognition for their work since e-print servers lack the same prestige as the established peer-reviewed print journals. Even science librarians, who are quick to embrace new information technologies, expressed concern about the inherent instability of electronic documents, since alteration and removal are simple tasks, and the uncertainty that digital collections will satisfactorily fulfill the archival role to the same standard as paper and other formats.

One of the concerns that fuel the resistance is the perceived loss of quality control since prior review and filtering is not required, or even available, in most e-print servers. Scientific research requires balancing the desire to be recognized as the first to discover or announce a particular idea and the need to ensure that the intellectual processes involved in studying this idea are appropriate, viable, and correct. Opponents of e-prints claim that this instantaneous type of publishing caters too much to this desire for primacy and, as a result, the scientific community will be flooded with poor research results. In particular, the biomedical and bio-chemical communities are concerned that premature or commercially slanted reports of discoveries in their fields could not only misinform or confuse the readers but also harm society (Kassirer and Angell 1995, Relman 1999). Bioscientists' concerns about the dangers of premature disclosure were so intense that even the influential National Institutes of Health were unable to garner enough support in the research community to create an E-biosci e-print server that would accept non-peer reviewed materials. The journal industry has put the research community's fear of information overload due to an increase in poor research at the center of their opposition to e-prints, and they strive to portray themselves as pro-tectors of research integrity and purity.

The issue of quality control and peer review is so contentious that even the staunchest advocates of e-print systems are divided in their perspec-tives on how to handle it. On one extreme, Harnad believes that the cur-rent system of peer review should continue unchanged in the transition from print to electronic publishing (Harnad 1996). On the other extreme, Ginsparg contends that peer review is a superfluous convention needed primarily to validate research and that the fear of ruining one's profes-sional reputation will prevent someone from submitting poorly devel-oped manuscripts to an e-print archive (Ginsparg 1994). Instead, Ginsparg sees more value in a post-publication, peer commentary system in which anyone, presumably with appropriate academic credentials, in-terested enough to write reviews or comments on an e-print may do so, and the comments will be directly linked to that e-print and viewable by the public as well. Andrew Odlyzko, a mathematician and cryptographer at AT&T Labs, suggests a compromise system that parallels the "schol-arly skywriting" vision proposed by Harnad in 1990 and synthesizes ele-ments from the traditional and open commentary systems (Odlyzko 1995). Odlyzko's proposal suggests that e-print archives implement a fil-ter that verifies appropriateness of topic and basic scholarly soundness to keep the obviously flawed items from appearing in the archive but then allows the submission, review, and revision of draft manuscripts that pass the filtration. This issue is far from resolved.

WHERE ARE WE NOW?

Even though e-print servers have not destroyed the journal industry, they have changed scholarly scientific communication significantly. Scholars in the fields that pioneered the transition to e-print archives now consider e-prints crucial to effective information sharing with colleagues around the world. E-prints have become so ingrained in the scholarly discourse of some disciplines that their cessation is quite unlikely due to the uproar such an action would cause in the research community. The freedom and ease of communication via e-prints is loosening the firm grip the journal industry held in scientific publishing and returning some control back to the authors.

Even though the number of e-print servers being established around the world each year has tapered off since the early 1990s, the electronic archives that have been created continue to expand and mature. Many science disciplines now have e-print servers of their own, largely modeled after *arXive*, and the pioneer servers have continued looking for ways to improve their products. Recently a group of e-print service experts started a movement to standardize the organization, search, retrieval, and delivery of e-prints across servers and disciplines. Because many of the pioneer servers were built on proprietary systems, seamless navigation and transfer between them was impossible. In 1999 a group of computer scientists, physicists, librarians, and other e-print experts met in New Mexico to discuss how to achieve interoperability among scholarly e-print sites. The "Santa Fe Convention" concluded with the development of the Open Archives Initiative (OAI), which defines the operational standards and framework for all future e-print development (Van de Sompel and Lagoze 2000). OAI has grown in the last few years and the endorsement by the Scholarly Publishing and Academic Resources Coalition (SPARC) <http://www.arl.org/sparc/> has ensured that the e-print remains an important part of scientific communication reform.

Also, since e-prints have not killed off any journal, publishers have begun to reconsider their position on them. While many continue to ban manuscripts previously released on e-print servers, several high-profile titles such as *Nature*, the *Lancet*, and the *British Medical Journal* have accepted the e-print as merely another form of scientific communication, and exposure on such servers does not necessarily pre-empt consideration for publication. Several publishers have even incorporated e-print servers into their manuscript submission and routing procedures. For instance, in 1996 the American Physical Society (APS) opened its own short-lived e-print server to function as the first step in the submission process to its journals (Taubes 1996b), and in early 2000 the commercial publishing giant Elsevier Science opened its *ChemWeb* <http://www.chemweb.com> preprint server to give chemists an opportunity to explore the role of e-print servers in scholarly communication and article preparation. E-prints even gained a foothold in the indexing and abstracting tools vital to basic research when ISI-Thomson Scientific began including preprint and e-print citations in their *Web of Science* files, and the American Chemical Society's Chemical Abstracts Services (CAS) division began selective indexing of the *arXive* files in its products. So even though publishers felt threatened by the introduction of e-prints into scientific discourse, they recognize that the e-print is thoroughly integrated into information sharing among scientists and are adapting to this reality.

E-PRINTS AND SCIENCE LIBRARIANS

It is clear that e-print services have grown from humble beginnings to become a force in shaping the future of scholarly publishing. E-print and other electronic archiving systems have had significant effects on scientific communication and journals, and, as a result, impact fundamentally the role of the science librarian. Some e-print advocates predict the end of libraries due to the increasing availability and reliability of digital alternatives of storing and retrieving scholarship (Odlyzko 1995). While this may be the case, or at least is a real possibility for the future, it is unlikely to happen soon. Until then, science librarians must take this opportunity to incorporate e-prints into their collections while they are still in their early stages and adapt library services to include the new communication format.

First, science librarians, especially those in research libraries, should increase the presence and visibility of e-print servers in their organizations. For smaller institutions merely listing the Internet addresses for the servers on library web pages may be sufficient, but more extensive steps are necessary for the larger research library. For instance, bibliographic instructors may create a module on e-print archive searching and discuss not only the navigational tools found in each server but also how to differentiate the reviewed and non-reviewed materials deposited there. Also, they may develop instructional modules in which they teach scholars how to use the various word processing and layout design applications recognized by the server systems.

Also most researchers are keenly aware of their time and are concerned with how much time they spend outside of the laboratory and away from "real" research. As a result, librarians, particularly in non-academic research institutions, frequently function as research consultants and conduct literature review and analysis of the results on the scientist's behalf. As a consultant, the research librarian must have in-depth knowledge not only of the search and retrieval protocols for a particular e-print archive but also how to navigate from one system to another. Additionally, the consulting librarian may assist researchers in putting manuscripts in proper format for e-print submission and maintaining the archive databases.

Science librarians should also become more active in e-print development by participating in the OAI and historical archive projects like the Public Library of Science <http://www.publiclibraryofscience.org/>. Librarians can influence the OAI by taking advantage of their knowledge of user information seeking and interface design to ensure that the e-print servers of the future not only are interoperable, but also easily navigable, intuitive, and aesthetically appealing to users. Another way in which librarians may promote the OAI is by creating and maintaining e-print archives within their institutions using the interoperability standards. These institutional servers not only will facilitate the dissemination of information created by local scholars in any discipline but also ensure the preservation of these documents through duplication. Librarian involvement in the Public Library of Science movement provides the opportunity to influence the design standards used to create stable electronic archives into which those e-prints that underwent peer review and publication in a journal may be placed and preserved for posterity.

CONCLUSION

The future of scientific publishing and communication is unclear since e-print advocates and supporters of the status quo are still debating the issues. No matter what the future holds, however, science librarians must use astute judgment and actively engage themselves in the process to ensure that free and open scholarly communication continues and that the scholarly record is preserved.

REFERENCES

Bouton, E.N. and S. Stevens-Rayburn. 1995. The Preprint Perplex in an Electronic Age. *Vistas in Astronomy* 39: 149-154.
Dallman, D., M. Draper and S. Schwarz. 1994. Electronic Pre-publishing for Worldwide Access: The Case of High Energy Physics. *Interlending & Document Supply* 22 (2): 3-7.

Davis, James R. and Carl Lagoze. 2000. NCSTRL: Design and Deployment of a Globally Distributed Digital Library. *Journal of the American Association for Information Science* 51 (3): 273-280.

Fjällbrant, Nancy. 1997. Scholarly communication–historical development and new possibilities. *IATUL Proceedings* 7: <http://educate.lib.chalmers.se/IATUL/proceed contents/fullpaper/nfpaper.html>.

Ginsparg, Paul. 1994. First Steps Towards Electronic Research Communication. *Computers in Physics* 8 (4): 390-296.

Harnad, Stevan. 1990. Scholarly Skywriting and the Prepublication Continuum of Scientific Inquiry. *Psychological Science* 1 (6): 342-344. <http://cogsci.soton.ac.uk/~harnad/Papers/Harnad/harnad90.skywriting.html>.

_____. 1996. Implementing Peer Review on the Net: Scientific Quality Control in Scholarly Electronic Journals. In *Scholarly Publication: The Electronic Frontier*, edited by Robin P. Peek and Gregory B. Newby. Cambridge, MA: MIT Press. <http://cogsci.soton.ac.uk/~harnad/Papers/Harnad/harnad96.peer.review.html>.

Kassirer, Jerome P. and Marcia Angell. 1995. The Internet and the *Journal. New England Journal of Medicine* 332 (25): 1709-1710.

Odlyzko, Andrew M. 1995. Tragic Loss or Good Riddance?: The Impending Demise of Traditional Scholarly Journals. *International Journal of Human Computer Studies* 42 (1): 71-122.

Okerson, Anne S., and James J. O'Donnell, eds. 1995. *Scholarly Journals at the Crossroads: A Subversive Proposal for Electronic Publishing*. Washington, DC: Association of Research Libraries.

Parker, Edwin B. 1971. *SPIRES (Stanford Public Information REtrieval System) 1970-71 Annual Report to the National Science Foundation*. Palo Alto, CA: Stanford University. [ERIC Microfiche ED 057828]

Relman, Arnold S. 1999. The NIH 'E-biomed' Proposal–A Potential Threat to the Evaluation and Orderly Dissemination of New Clinical Studies. *New England Journal of Medicine* 340 (23): 1828-1829.

Taubes, Gary. 1993. Publication by Electronic Mail Takes Physics by Storm. *Science* 259 (5099): 1246-1248.

_____. 1996a. Electronic Preprints Point the Way to 'Author Empowerment.' *Science* 271 (5250): 767-768.

_____. 1996b. APS Starts Electronic Preprint Service. *Science* 273 (5273): 304.

Till, James E. 2001. Predecessors of preprint servers. *Learned Publishing* 14 (1): 7-13.

Van de Sompel, Herbert and Carl Lagoze. 2000. The Santa Fe Convention of the Open Archives Initiative. *D-Lib Magazine* 6 (2): <http://www.dlib.org/dlib/february00/vandesompel-oai/02vandesompel-oai.html>.

Youngen, Gregory K. 1998. Citation Patterns to Traditional and Electronic Preprints in the Published Literature. *College & Research Libraries* 59 (5): 448-456.

ELECTRONIC SERVICES

Bringing the Human Touch
to Digital Library Services

Deborah L. Helman

SUMMARY. Since the evolution of the World Wide Web, the presence of libraries and their resources has grown at a dramatic pace. Increasingly, the users of this information are primarily accessing library resources remotely. While libraries have put many collections and services online, most are just beginning to plan services that will provide similar real-time assistance currently available at library service desks. The MIT Libraries' experience with providing real-time digital reference has been extremely well received by users, which in addition has led to a 52% increase in email reference service. It has revealed a variety of technical challenges. The greater, long-term challenges revealed, however, are staff-related. *[Article copies available for a fee from The Haworth Document Delivery Service: 1-800-HAWORTH. E-mail address: <getinfo@haworthpressinc.com> Website: <http://www.HaworthPress.com> © 2001 by The Haworth Press, Inc. All rights reserved.]*

KEYWORDS. Digital reference, real-time digital reference, live assistance, live help

Deborah L. Helman, BS (Electrical Engineering), MLS, is Associate Head and Reference Coordinator, Barker Engineering Library, Massachusetts Institute of Technology, Cambridge, MA.

[Haworth co-indexing entry note]: "Bringing the Human Touch to Digital Library Services." Helman, Deborah L. Co-published simultaneously in *Science & Technology Libraries* (The Haworth Information Press, an imprint of The Haworth Press, Inc.) Vol. 20, No. 2/3, 2001, pp. 83-96; and: *Electronic Resources and Services in Sci-Tech Libraries* (ed: Mary C. Schlembach, and William H. Mischo) The Haworth Information Press, an imprint of The Haworth Press, Inc., 2001, pp. 83-96. Single or multiple copies of this article are available for a fee from The Haworth Document Delivery Service [1-800-HAWORTH, 9:00 a.m. - 5:00 p.m. (EST). E-mail address: getinfo@haworthpressinc.com].

INTRODUCTION

Many libraries established their presence on the Internet early on. Since the evolution of the World Wide Web (WWW), however, the presence of libraries and their resources and other information sources has grown at an ever-quickening pace. We are continually adding more databases and full-text collections (both journals and books), as well as services, such as a variety of service request forms, instructional tutorials, and desktop delivery of materials. Increasingly, our users access our online collections and services anywhere and anytime. This has enabled many users to access the library remotely for most of their information needs. At the Massachusetts Institute of Technology (MIT), the evidence of this is shown with our in-library reference statistics and door counts going down, while use of our Web site and online services have increased dramatically.

As collections and other collections-related services have been put online in greater number, digital reference services have also been made available online. Most libraries today have email reference services, to provide an asynchronous interaction with users, subject guides and pathfinders, and instructional tutorials. On occasion, our remote users still need the human touch we provide at the reference desk and in order to best serve our users, libraries must find an effective way to provide real-time reference service to these remote users, while balancing the needs of our in-library users. This paper will discuss MIT's project to bring the human touch in real-time to our digital library services and what we have learned about the technical and staffing challenges in providing real-time digital reference.

THE MIT LIBRARIES DIGITAL REFERENCE PROJECT

For many years MIT Libraries have been providing email reference service, which has seen increasing popularity every year. In the early 90s (before the WWW,) we also had a somewhat unsuccessful brush with a "chat" enabled service in conjunction with MIT's Information Services department provided over the Internet. Inspired by some of the exciting projects discussed, and new and developing technologies demonstrated in 1999 at the Virtual Reference Desk (VRD) Conference, the MIT Libraries set out to try again and develop a real-time, Web-based digital reference service.

In January 2000, a team was formed to analyze the technologies that existed and create a proposal for an experimental digital reference service, which later gained support from the MIT Libraries' administration. In the Spring of 2000, key players in real-time online customer center software were identified (Nash 1999): Cisco's Webline, LivePerson, Sneakerlabs' iServe, eShare's NetAgent, Videogate [now Convey Systems], eGain Live, Lotus Sametime, FaceTime, iSession/Instant Service. (Note: many new products are now available and we no longer consider all of these major players.) Product criteria were developed (see Figure 1) and four products (Cisco's Webline, LivePerson, Sneakerlabs' iserve, and eShare's NetAgent) were evaluated in depth against these criteria. After recommending one product in late Spring of 2000, we ultimately chose Library Systems & Services' (LSSI) new Virtual Reference Software (VRS) (http://www.lssi.com) due to the company's library focus, forming a developmental relationship with LSSI for the initial phases of this project.

The project team recommended that MIT Libraries do a pilot project with four major goals. First and foremost, we wanted to explore these new technologies, with the following in mind: determining what the tech-

FIGURE 1. Criteria for Evaluating Customer Center Software

High Priority

- Easy to use for customer
- Platform/browser independent
- Globally accessible
- One-to-one conversations (private)
- Ability to refer/transfer users to another agent
- Co-browsing and/or ability to "push" Web pages
- Alert for agent and/or paging of agents when customer requests service
- Ability to provide access to MIT secured resources (databases, ejournals, etc.) whether user is on- or off-campus
- Archived transcripts of transactions (searchable)
- Privacy of the archive
- Ability to restrict to MIT user community

Very Desirable

- Ability to customize an "away message" for down times/holidays/etc.
- Ability for agent to have simultaneous conversations
- Skills routing–ability to route questions by skill/subject
- No advertising
- One-to-many conversations–ability for one agent to "talk" to more than one customer at a time
- Ability to place a user on "hold"

nology has to offer now and for the future; evaluating how the technology works in MIT's complex computing environment; determining what is lacking in the current technology/product; and evaluating LSSI's Virtual Reference Software against the other continually developing products in this fast-paced market. We also wanted to assess the service from both the user's and the staff's perspectives. We needed to determine if real-time digital reference service served a user need, and if that need exists, when the best time to offer the service would be and how best to publicize it. On the staff side, we wanted to take the opportunity to explore different staffing models, evaluate training needs and find out where the service is best staffed. The final goal of this pilot project was to evaluate the technical and administrative support needs for maintaining such a service.

During the Summer and Fall of 2000, ten librarians were recruited from all five of the major subject-based libraries at MIT to staff Ask Us!–Live, as we call our new real-time digital reference service. After training and service customization in November/December 2000, the service went live in late January 2001. Ask Us!–Live became MIT's only "general" reference point, creating special training issues, which will be discussed later. When introduced, Ask Us!–Live was available two hours a day (Monday-Friday, 2pm-4pm,) while we learned more about how this technology worked in our computing environment and explored the staffing implications of creating an additional service point. The service is available to the entire MIT community (on- and off-campus), as well as non-MIT, on-campus users. Initially links to Ask Us!–Live were placed on only a few strategic pages (the Libraries' catalog, the databases/ejournals page, and our research assistance page) and in the first few months publicity was limited to targeted user communities, while staff became familiar with providing reference service in this new environment.

Ask Us!–Live has met with a very positive reaction from our user community. User feedback has been very enthusiastic–provided to librarians during our online sessions and through a survey–even when there has been major technical problems! For example:

> "By the way, I think this new LIVE thing is absolutely great"
>
> "Interesting service–I like [the] personal touch. Thanks again."
>
> "I hope that you are able to extend the hours soon. This is my preferred method of interacting with library staff."
>
> "Ask Us!–Live is amazing. The librarian was helpful and nice."
>
> "Great service! Definitely a keeper."

In just over six months of service we have answered over 175 questions. Service has continually grown, even during the summer months. An unexpected side effect of introducing Ask Us!–Live has been a significant increase in our e-mail reference questions due to referrals made to the e-mail service when the live service is closed. In the first six months of service, e-mail reference increased by 75% compared to the same 6 months the previous year and by 52% compared to the 6 months prior to introducing Ask Us!–Live. Based on a survey of users of our service (MIT Libraries 2001), 28 of 29 responded that they would use this service again. Users also expressed an interest in seeing this service available from 9am to 9pm (see Figure 2). When users were asked when they would be most likely to use Ask Us!–Live, most users (38 %) preferred 12pm to 3pm, while 3pm to 6pm was a close second (28%). Also of note from the survey, 27 of 29 have used the reference desk before. While users seem to have received this service with open arms, there are many challenges that we have faced, both technical and staff-related.

CHALLENGES

While there have been some technical challenges, the most significant are primarily due to the developing nature of co-browsing technology and learning how this new technology works (or does not) in our current digital environment. At the time of this writing, LSSI's Virtual Reference

FIGURE 2. Results of Ask Us!–Live User Survey (Spring 2001-August 11, 2001)

Time of Day	I would like Ask Us!–Live to be available . . . (select all that apply)		I would be most likely to use Ask Us!–Live . . . (select only one)	
	# (29 total)	%	# (29 total)	%
Midnight-3am	0	0	0	0
3am-6am	0	0	0	0
6am-9am	1	3	0	0
9am-Noon	19	66	1	3
Noon-3pm	20	69	11	38
3pm-6pm	18	62	8	28
6pm -9pm	18	62	5	17
9pm-Midnight	7	24	4	14

Software currently uses the eGain Live software. It is hosted remotely by LSSI, so MIT Libraries has not had to confront the technical and support issues that arise when hosting the service on a local server. However, the remote hosting of Ask Us!–Live has brought to bear a different range of issues. Following are some key technical issues we have confronted and what we have done to address them.

Co-Browsing Databases and Web Sites

The co-browsing feature of this and other similar technologies is one of the features which makes this technology so alluring to libraries. When co-browsing, the librarian's and the user's browsers are synchronized, enabling the librarian to show a user how to do a search, create a better search statement, fill out a form together and more. The librarian and user fundamentally share a Web browser, with both user and librarian able to interact with the Web page. Getting this to actually work for us was one of our greatest challenges. Initially, LSSI's VRS had limitations on how it interacted with proprietary databases. As LSSI began to resolve the many issues with co-browsing databases, MIT Libraries had to get our proxy server (EZproxy) to work with LSSI's VRS for this to function properly. At the time of this writing, LSSI has gotten many of the databases to function with their co-browsing software and continue to work on resolving the issues with those that don't. MIT Libraries, EZproxy and LSSI worked together to solve the issues with the proxy server and in August 2000 we began to use the co-browsing feature to search databases with our users.

Another issue that is yet unresolved and remains a stumbling block is the tendency of some Web sites to freeze, crash, or take over the entire browser of both the librarian and/or user. Types of Web sites that can cause such problems are: "frame-busting" sites (e.g., http://www.webhelp.com); secure sites; personalized sites (e.g., http://www.amazon.com); sites that "maintain state" (some library catalogs); sites that require users to have a plug-in; and sites that require certain types of authentication (LSSI 2001). Recoveries can be made when some of these problems occur by both the librarian and the user. If the user is not affected, the librarian is able to log back into the system and rejoin the session which was already in progress. In the event that a user is effected, recovery tips are provided upon entry, enabling the user to get back to the session as well. In order to avoid such circumstances, librarians try not to take users into uncharted territory and when they need to do so they often try new Web sites in a separate browser before leading a user there. When they are unable to take a user directly to a Web site, URLs are provided and screen shots of the Web sites can be sent by the librarian. However, this issue is related to browser technology and continues to be a problem with co-browsing software in general.

Limiting the Service to the MIT Community

We decided that we would limit this service to the MIT user community. However, we wanted to make this service available both on- and off-campus. We solved this problem by using our proxy server to authenticate our users in the same way that we do for the proprietary databases to which we provide access. When a user is on-campus they are passed through to the Ask Us!–Live login page, and if they are off-campus they are prompted for MIT certificates, which once provided they are then sent to the login page. MIT certificates are quite commonly used for secure access to MIT campus resources, with the only current limitation being that they only work in Netscape. MIT is currently developing certificates to work in Internet Explorer, so this should not be an issue for much longer.

Browser/Platform Compatibility

Users at MIT, as in most other academic environments, operate on every kind of computing platform and browser possible. LSSI's VRS supports the major browsers (Netscape/Internet Explorer) of customers using the service, with some lost functionality with earlier versions of browsers. Most of our users have not encountered problems, however we have found that some users on Macs and Unix do not come in with full functionality. We did, however, run into problems on the librarian's side. We found that our librarians needed to be on a PC, running Windows, and that they needed to be using Internet Explorer. While this was not a major issue, we did need to provide all of our librarians with Internet Explorer (we are primarily a Netscape campus) and one librarian who worked on a Mac, now was in the position of having to borrow a colleague's computer during her hours on Ask Us!–Live. All other Ask Us!–Live staff found that staffing Ask Us!–Live from their computer has given them an opportunity to be very productive between questions and this librarian was now unable to reap these benefits.

Speed/Reliability over the Internet

Effective, quality co-browsing relies on the speed and reliability of the Internet. The better your connection to the server, the lower the probability that problems will occur in your interaction with users. We have found that, on occasion, this can be an issue, and is something that users need to be made aware of.

While there have been some technical challenges, many of these have been relatively easy to resolve over time or will be as the technology continues to develop. The MIT Libraries' far greater challenge has been and will continue to be staff-related issues: time to devote to planning, implementing and managing Ask Us!–Live, deployment of human resources to provide service, buy-in, training, referrals, and technical support.

Time

Planning and implementing this service has taken longer than expected and has also taken more staff time than predicted. MIT Libraries took about a year from the early stages of exploration until actually going live with our service. From discussions with other libraries providing real-time digital reference, we have learned that as a product gains functionality and customizability, there is much more administrative time needed, particularly during the implementation phase. During the implementation phase, the Ask Us!–Live management team and systems staff did the following: co-browsing functionality was tested and made operational; scripted messages and URLs were written; system customizations were made, including system messages (welcome/closed, etc.); queues for routing questions based on subject were developed; customer entry pages for the MIT Libraries' Web site were designed; logos for the Ask Us!–Live service were created; and staff were trained. This needed to be done just to get the service up and running. While not requiring the same attention on an ongoing basis, these are all tasks that will need to be maintained and developed in the future.

Doing a pilot project enabled us to go live with the service, providing a limited service (2 hours a day), while we developed Ask Us!–Live and learned about call center technologies and how the MIT community would take advantage of them. The pilot nature of this project, while still time consuming, reduced the overall impact on staff time, while giving us the opportunity to obtain experience with providing real-time digital reference and to observe staffing issues that arise in adding such a service. Ask Us!–Live represents a sixth major reference service point, that needs staff to allocate time to providing the live service and to managing it–someone to provide a schedule, organize training for staff, and assess the service on a continual basis. We have learned if we are to expand and enhance Ask Us!–Live, we need to begin a serious review of staffing models. Our greatest challenge will be to develop a staffing model, which will allow us to sustain and scale this service.

Human Resources

How we will continue to staff Ask Us!–Live is an issue we struggle with and are just beginning to seriously explore. Currently, the Ask Us!–Live staff and project management team have all taken this on as an additional responsibility. As we begin to discuss expansion of the service, we realize that this is not a sustainable model and alternative ways to deploy our human resources must be sought. At Cornell's Olin, Kroch and Uris Libraries, for instance, they employ dedicated reference assistants that assist in supporting all of their reference services–in-library, e-mail, and chat–providing an integrated and tiered approach to reference. Management of the Reference question is emphasized, with less experienced staff providing an "interactive real-time digital sign post" (Skipper 2001), referring users to an expert when the question requires a more in-depth answer. This is one approach and there are many others. MIT will begin to explore the pros and cons of some of the following ideas in the near future: replace five staffed in-library service points with one or two librarians available online during specified hours; station information staff at reference and/or circulation desks, while librarians are available online and for research consultations; train information staff to triage questions and refer to experts as needed. Every one of these models impacts support staff and the question of fair compensation will have to be considered. There will not be one right answer. Every library setting will need to see what works in their environment and for their users. We do know, however, that how we deploy our staff will need to change and that all public services staff will need to be involved in designing our new staffing model.

Buy-In

When introducing any new service, getting buy-in is of key importance. As we look towards the future, we need both support from the library administration and other staff. Library administration need to be able to support this service, both with resources to fund the purchase of this software, as well as the human resources to staff it, and we have tried to provide them with the information needed to do so. We have had an ongoing online user survey for most of the pilot phase, which users were directed to upon logout. The user survey allowed us to gain both feedback to support the need for this service, as well as other information that will help us improve our service in general. We have also surveyed the Ask Us!–Live staff to get their views on how this service has filled our users' needs and to gain insight into how this has impacted service on their other work and the work of their local units. During various phases of this project, we have also had discussions with our Public Services Management Group to gain their support for the continuing development of Ask Us!–Live. However, in order for this service to become fully integrated into our package of services, library staff must support it and we need to build a shared vision for this service. We have held a series of discussions, both in all staff meetings and local staff meetings to begin discussing digital reference and how it fits into the package of services provided at the MIT Libraries. We will continue to build on these discussions as we move forward and begin looking at new staffing models for expanded service.

Training

Providing training has been of key importance in rolling out Ask Us!–Live and librarians attended a series of training sessions. Initially, all librarians staffing Ask Us!–Live were trained on how to use the software. LSSI's Virtual Reference Software is a fairly easy product to use, but there are many features to learn and hands-on practice has been stressed. Librarians were paired up to practice with each other, enabling them to learn what they needed to know as the librarian, as well as what it was like to be the user, which proved to be very important. Chat skills (Ronan 2001) are also extremely important in real-time digital reference. We have found that other libraries already providing chat reference services have had an easier move to more full-featured products like VRS because their chat skills had already been developed. We were taking a greater leap, and thus needed more training and practice with our chat skills. Doing real-time digital reference requires that you also remember to use your reference interview skills in the chat environment, which is initially hard to remember. Over time, the Ask Us!–Live staff has seen their chat skills and ability to do reference in the digital environment improve dramatically.

As mentioned before, the "general" reference nature of Ask Us!–Live posed a special training need–our librarians needed cross-training in our different subject specialties. Our engineering librarians were to find that they would be asked questions about the French writer, Marcel Proust, and our humanities librarians would be asked about materials properties. We set up a series of cross-training sessions to cover the basics of each broad subject area. Our goal was to give the Ask Us!–Live staff enough knowledge to make them feel comfortable enough to answer basic questions and refer users to the right person if they were unable to answer the question. We continue to do cross-training and must continue to expand this in order to provide a more extensive live service.

Referrals

Referrals have become a core part of Ask Us!–Live primarily because of the general reference nature of this service, but also due in part to the limitations of working in a digital environment (no print resources, some questions too complex, etc.) The majority of questions can be answered on the spot. However, as at the in-library reference desk, there are always questions that need a different level of expertise and should be referred. When librarians get to the point of referral, they will let the user know who they are referring the question to and will upon receipt of the transcript of the session forward it to someone who will be able to answer the question. The challenge that we faced here was quite unexpected. During discussions about Ask Us!–Live with both our branch librarians and the Institute Archives staff, none of whom were participating directly in the pilot project, concern was expressed that Ask Us!–Live staff would not appropriately refer questions to them which related to their subject expertise. This concern, however, was not expressed in regard to our physical reference desks, which have faced the issue of referral for ages. We have approached this challenge as a training opportunity. During Fall 2001, the Archives staff will do a session for all public services staff on what services they provide so that we are better equipped to refer questions to them. We will also be including referrals as part of the cross-training all Ask Us!–Live staff receive. This issue also relates to buy-in–our challenge is to get these concerned staff to help us build a shared vision of how Ask Us!–Live integrates with all of our library services.

Technical Support

Finally, another major challenge that we face with this and many other projects, is finding staff who can support and lead the development of a technology based service on a daily basis. Not only do we need the basic technical support from our systems staff, who are already spread thin, we also need a leader on our project management team to analyze the technical problems we face and to work closely with both the LSSI technical support team and our own systems staff to solve the day-to-day problems which arise. As customer center software continually develops, staff will need to be identified to fill this role so that we can stay at the forefront of this field.

NEXT STEPS AT THE MIT LIBRARIES

While we continue to grapple with the many challenges addressed above, we have committed to developing and expanding this service. During Fall 2001, we have gained administrative support to expand and change our service hours. Six new librarians eagerly joined the Ask Us!–Live staff, allowing us to offer an extra hour of service daily (Mon-Thurs, 3pm-6pm, Fri, 3-5pm). One librarian will now staff Ask Us!–Live from 5pm-6pm, serving all the libraries, rather than having multiple service desks staffed by as many librarians. We will also be experimenting with closing the reference desk from 12pm-1pm in one library, with circulation staff trained to provide information service in place of the reference staff. We will continue to experiment with staffing models as we plan for future expansion of Ask Us!–Live.

In order to make decisions about what the future of digital reference in the MIT Libraries should be, we have come to realize we need to develop a shared vision for how real-time digital reference service integrates into the service package we want to provide to the MIT community, now and in the future. In order to do this, we must create a new vision for reference services at MIT Libraries, where real-time digital reference is one of many services we wish to provide. We must decide if this is a complementary service or a replacement service. Over the course of the next six months to a year, all public services staff will be involved in discussing the future of reference service and its impact on both staff and users. Users will also be further engaged in discussion about how they would like to see this service develop, with both a new online user survey and a series of focus groups.

Continued evaluation of the product field also took place in Fall/Winter 2001/2002. We have learned a great deal since our initial review of call center software that will help us to look at all available products in a more critical fashion. The digital reference project team has begun to re-evaluate our criteria for product selection and will apply these criteria to the product field as it stands today in order to select the product that will best support MIT Libraries' vision for reference services.

CONCLUSION

While libraries will continue to face many challenges, both technical and staff-related, in regard to implementing the quickly developing call center technologies, we must not be stymied by them. Libraries continue to experiment with the technology and we must challenge ourselves to look differently at how we staff these and other services. Many more libraries take on these challenges every day as they begin to bring that human touch to the digital world. There is an excitement about the possibilities for the future of reference that brings librarians from everywhere to enthusiastically share their visions for digital reference and their experiences with the many challenges inherent in providing this service. Librarians must continue this dialogue and work together to solve these problems. Some libraries are already working to do so by exploring collaborative service arrangements to provide extended service, such as the Library of Congress' well-known Collaborative Digital Reference Service (CDRS) (Library of Congress 2001). MIT Libraries looks forward to exploring the potential of such relationships–can collaborative service relationships, whether library system to library system or arranged topically (Lankes conversation 2001), be a piece of the staffing solution to providing digital reference service 24/7? This and many other questions are still left to be answered. Digital reference has given us an opportunity to interact with users in a way that they often find fun, convenient and extremely useful. We must seize this opportunity to reconnect with our users online, designing reference services for the future.

FOR MORE INFORMATION ON DIGITAL REFERENCE

1. To read more, see Bernie Sloan's extensive bibliographies of articles related to the provision of reference services in a digital environment, including e-mail, chat, and co-browsing.

Sloan, Bernie. (2000, November 7) Digital reference services: a bibliography. Retrieved on 22 August 2001 from the Graduate School of Library and Information Science, University of Illinois at Urbana-Champaign's Web site: <http://www.lis.uiuc.edu/%7Eb-sloan/digiref.html>.

Sloan, Bernie. (2001, July 19) Digital reference services bibliography: a supplement. Retrieved on 22 August 2001 from the Graduate

School of Library and Information Science, University of Illinois at Urbana-Champaign's Web site: <http://alexia.lis.uiuc.edu/~b-sloan/bibsupp.htm>.

2. The Virtual Reference Desk (VRD) Conference

http://www.vrd.org

The VRD conferences are a wonderful place to learn about the latest trends in digital reference and discuss the issues with other librarians providing digital reference. VRD is sponsored by The Virtual Reference Desk (VRD) Project, which is "dedicated to the advancement of digital reference and the successful creation and operation of human-mediated, Internet-based information services" (Kasowitz 2000).

3. Join the DIG_REF listserv (Lankes 2001), sponsored by VRD

http://www.vrd.org/Dig_Ref/dig_ref.shtml

DIG_REF is a listserv that brings together librarians and other information professionals providing reference services via the Internet.

REFERENCES

Kasowitz, A. and Bennett, B. (2000, September 27) About VRD. Retrieved on 22 August 2001 from the Virtual Reference Desk Web site: <http://www.vrd.org/about.shtml>.

Lankes conversation June 21, 2001 at MIT, David Lankes introduced the concept of topical collaborative service arrangements.

Lankes, R.D. DIG_REF Listserv. Retrieved on 22 August 2001 from the Virtual Reference Desk Web site: <http://www.vrd.org/Dig_Ref/dig_ref.shtml>.

Library of Congress. (2001, August 14) Collaborative Digital Reference Service (CDRS) Retrieved on 22 August 2001 from the Collaborative Digital Reference Service Web site: <http://www.loc.gov/rr/digiref/>.

LSSI. (2001) Virtual reference services training workbook, p. 29.

MIT Libraries survey data, Ask Us!–Live: User Survey, Spring 2001, as of 8/11/2001.

Nash, S. (1999) Real-time help. PC Magazine, December 22. Retrieved on 22 August 2001 from the ZDNet Reviews Web site: <http://www.zdnet.com/products/stories/reviews/0,4161,2408774,00.html>.

Ronan, J. (2001, May 7) RefXpress Chat Communication Tips. Retrieved on 22 August 2001 from the University of Florida Libraries Web site: <http://www.uflib.ufl.edu/hss/ref/rxchat.html>.

Skipper, N. Digital dominoes: the impact of digital reference on the traditional reference model. ACRL 10th National Conference, March 15-18, 2001, Denver, CO.

Re-Envisioning Instruction
for the Electronic Environment
of a 21st Century
Science-Engineering Library

Marianne Stowell Bracke
Lori Jean Critz

SUMMARY. Library services have changed dramatically in recent years due to the rapid developments in both information technology and electronic resources. The behavior and expectations of users have changed as well. Users expect to find full-text information online that is retrievable with a minimum of effort. The information literacy movement is influencing the approaches of many instruction librarians, but this influence is often realized in generic materials geared to reach the greatest number of students, materials that do not suit the specific needs of science and engineering library customers. Librarians must re-envision instruction for an environment where a "one size fits all" approach is not appropriate. *[Article copies available for a fee from The Haworth Document Delivery Service: 1-800-HAWORTH. E-mail address: <getinfo@haworth pressinc.com> Website: <http://www.HaworthPress.com> © 2001 by The Haworth Press, Inc. All rights reserved.]*

KEYWORDS. Library instruction, information literacy, serendipity, undergraduate students

Marianne Stowell Bracke, BA (History), MS (Library and Information Science), and Lori Jean Critz, MS (Microbiology), MLIS, are both Assistant Librarians, Science-Engineering Library, University of Arizona, Tucson, AZ.

[Haworth co-indexing entry note]: "Re-Envisioning Instruction for the Electronic Environment of a 21st Century Science-Engineering Library." Bracke, Marianne Stowell, and Lori Jean Critz. Co-published simultaneously in *Science & Technology Libraries* (The Haworth Information Press, an imprint of The Haworth Press, Inc.) Vol. 20, No. 2/3, 2001, pp. 97-106; and: *Electronic Resources and Services in Sci-Tech Libraries* (ed: Mary C. Schlembach, and William H. Mischo) The Haworth Information Press, an imprint of The Haworth Press, Inc., 2001, pp. 97-106. Single or multiple copies of this article are available for a fee from The Haworth Document Delivery Service [1-800-HAWORTH, 9:00 a.m. - 5:00 p.m. (EST). E-mail address: getinfo@haworthpressinc.com].

INTRODUCTION

Library services have changed dramatically in recent years due to the rapid developments in both information technology and electronic resources. The behavior and expectations of undergraduate users have changed as well. These users expect to find full-text information online that is retrievable with a minimum of effort. Increasingly, libraries are focused on information literacy instruction as a means of preparing users to navigate and evaluate electronic resources effectively. Information literacy instruction often is delivered during lower-level undergraduate courses and is concentrated on teaching similarities among resources in order to reach the broadest number of students. However, through the course of their academic careers science and engineering undergraduates develop unique information needs that are not always well met through a generalized approach to teaching information literacy. In this essay, the authors discuss how science and engineering librarians should re-envision instruction in order to provide a more individualized system of instruction that accounts for these students' status as modern undergraduates and science and engineering majors.

SCIENCE AND ENGINEERING UNDERGRADUATE STUDENTS

Many of today's traditional undergraduate students (the eighteen through twenty-something group) have grown up with computers integrated into everyday and academic life. Computer use among incoming freshmen is at an all-time high (Kellogg 2001). Moreover, these students are motivated by and focused on the outcomes of their education. For example, the 2000 Freshman Survey by UCLA's Higher Education Research Institute indicated that over eighty percent of incoming freshmen plan on obtaining a graduate degree. Seventy percent cited the desire to make more money as a motivation to attend college, and over seventy-one percent cited the need to get profession-specific training or to be able to get a better job as a reason. In contrast, when considering what objectives are essential, less than forty percent cite influencing social values while sixteen percent cite the desire to make a theoretical contribution to science. Only eighteen percent cite becoming involved in cleaning up the environment or influencing the political structure as very important objectives. In short, students' emphasis appears to be more self-focused and goal-oriented rather than outwardly focused, or focused on a quest for knowledge (Kellogg 2001).

In addition to what is known about today's undergraduates, there are some differences in academic activities and expectations for students in science and engineering disciplines that sets them apart from their peers. Course work in these majors tends to emphasize active hands-on participation in their learning experiences (e.g., project and lab-oriented assignments) for both individual and collaborative efforts. Hativa and Birenbaum indicate that students in engineering curricula are often required to use self-regulated learning approaches: "They are required to perform original and inventive individual projects and to frequently solve difficult problems on their own and generally to put more work and thinking effort into their assignments than education students" (Hativa and Birenbaum 2000).

Science and engineering majors also need to learn how to navigate within the increasingly complex electronic information environment. They must become proficient in basic information skills, which include: an understanding of the structure of information within the library's domain as well as outside it; the mechanics of information retrieval for varying information formats; and the evaluative competency needed to select the appropriate resources and options for a particular information need.

Of these information skills, evaluative competency is, perhaps, one of the most crucial and yet most complex skills for students to acquire. Students need to be able to distinguish between Web pages created by authors who may or may not be knowledgeable on a subject, and databases licensed by libraries, which are frequently the electronic counterpart to the reputable indexes libraries have relied upon for years. Users of Web search engines may encounter great difficulty, possibly unwittingly, in retrieving accurate information. A 1999 study of the AltaVista search engine indicate that only 27.2% of pages returned contained correct, or mostly correct, answers to the authors' questions, while incorrect or mostly incorrect information was found in 8.8% of returned pages (Connell and Tipple 1999). Faculty have accepted Web pages as a part of students' research, but frequently take steps to insure that students seek non-Web resources as well. These faculty report that often students display a lack of ability to evaluate resources, regardless of format (Herring 2001). Teaching of evaluative skills is essential and must extend to all types of resources, but is not the only necessary focus of information literacy instruction for science and engineering majors.

Science and engineering students need to master complex subject-specific resources that often require a sophisticated and diverse set of search skills. Competency is crucial to success in their chosen academic endeavors and will be applicable in their professional careers (Leckie and Fullerton 1999). The American Chemical Society's Committee on Professional Training stipulates that one primary objective of laboratory instruction is to give students "the self-confidence and competence to . . . plan and execute experiments through the use of the literature" (American Chemical Society 1999). Information literacy instruction for these students should, therefore, be specific, context-based, and highly relevant to their current information needs. Moreover, instruction efforts should address the desire expressed by science and engineering students to fulfill their information needs in the most convenient, comfortable, and time-saving manner possible (Brown 1999) by providing guidance on "shortcuts," quick tips, and alternatives to standard searching mechanics whenever possible.

In addition to the unique characteristics of these students, the expectations and philosophies of their faculty add an additional layer of complexity to teaching information literacy. Research has shown that while most faculty in these disciplines believe undergraduate students should be taught information literacy skills, the majority do not believe it is necessary to include information literacy in their classes (Hativa and Birenbaum 2000). Other faculty do not see it as their responsibility at all, claiming that undergraduates should already possess such skills (Leckie and Fullerton 1999). Additionally, science and engineering courses are often centered on standard textbooks for the first two, and sometimes even three, years of the undergraduate curriculum. Lower-division undergraduate science and engineering courses often do not rely on external library resources for coursework. Despite these factors, the students are still expected to have information literacy skills even though class time is not always provided to acquire these skills (Leckie and Fullerton 1999). This creates a situation in which undergraduate science and engineering students may not receive any information literacy training unless they receive it in general education or elective courses.

DELIVERY OF INSTRUCTION OUTSIDE THE CLASSROOM

Knowing that science and engineering undergraduates have needs for information literacy, librarians face the challenging task of finding ways to introduce information-seeking skills. As noted previously, course-integrated classroom opportunities are not always available–or even the preferred option for instruction. Many libraries have begun to explore online tutorials to reach these students, but little is yet known about their effectiveness for specific populations of students. Advancements in technology and the constantly improving Web skills of librarians allow tutorials to grow more complex and, to a degree, interactive. Unfortunately, most librarians lack the time, money, programming skills, and artistic flair necessary to make cutting edge Web tutorials. Tutorials are still primitive in comparison to the average video or Web game that is as common and ordinary to the undergraduate student as a microwave oven.

Furthermore, there has been little research assessing whether students can and will learn through online tutorials, or if they will use them without prompting from an instructor. Recent studies have confirmed what most instruction librarians already know: online tutorials cannot, and should not, be substituted for librarian interaction with students. Simply stated, "web-based library tutorials are best used in connection with academic classes rather than in isolation" (Dewald 1999). Additionally, many library tutorials are accessed in an artificial environment and are generic in nature, teaching catalog searching, basic search strategies, and other information literacy skills outside the student's learning context. Tutorials are frequently designed to send the user back and forth between the tutorial and the resource, rather than mimicking a more natural search process. Teaching out of context in an artificial environment may make it difficult, if not impossible, for students to acquire transferable skills.

Although online tutorials may have utility when face-to-face contact is not possible, or for those who prefer this type of instruction, instruction delivered in person is almost always optimal. An excellent face-to-face instruction opportunity is through a reference desk interaction. Ackerson states that "linking reference service (a reactive transaction) more closely with library instruction (a proactive transaction) can strengthen both activities and support more effective and consistent interaction . . . " (Ackerson 1996). In this setting, teaching traditional in-depth searching skills may be challenging due to the brevity of the interaction, especially when the goal is to teach transferable skills. It is important, however, to recognize these interactions as teachable moments in which information literacy skills may be taught immediately and within the context of a student's work.

Library patrons, undergraduates in particular, commonly come to the desk with skills and experience in using the Web. In fact, the 1998 UCLA Higher Education Research Institute Freshman Survey indicated that 82.9% of freshmen had used the Web for research or homework, a number that has surely risen in the succeeding years (Sax 1998). More often than not this means undergraduates have some experience with serendipitous searching, where results, whether correct or not, are found seemingly through chance. Although this method can seem random compared to focused Boolean searching, in actuality serendipitous searching is more targeted than it may appear. On the Web, and in free and licensed databases, links are rarely random. Links on Web pages often point to pages on related topics. Likewise, library databases (e.g., INSPEC or Science Citation Index) in which displayed records include hyperlinks often point to related information such as other articles by an author, other articles on a subject, or articles citing the article. A savvy user can utilize this structure to quickly navigate to potentially relevant information.

Knowing that many users have experience with serendipitous searching presents an opportunity to teach searching skills without relying exclusively on Boolean logic or crafting elaborate search strategies. Librarians can highlight and explain the value of special features available in Web-based databases, such as clickable subject headings or descriptors, thereby involving the user in the search immediately and building upon existing skills.

These special features appear more and more often in databases and can be a great aid in getting to specific information quickly. The National Library of Medicine's *Entrez* is a prime example of interconnectivity for serendipitous searching. With *Entrez*, users can search and retrieve data from eight databases produced by the National Center for Biotechnology Information. These linked databases allow users to pursue pertinent information as they encounter it. In another example, citation indexes (e.g., Science Citation Index), especially in hyperlinked format, lend themselves to serendipitous searching by providing links for cited authors, cited publications, or full-text within an individual record. Moreover, the linking of electronic resources through programs such as CrossRef provide mechanisms for chance encounters, by lending the "browsing of the stacks" feel to the electronic universe. In fact, CrossRef describes linking as enabling "readers to gain access to logically related articles with one or two clicks–an objective widely accepted among researchers as a natural and necessary part of scientific and scholarly publishing in the digital age." These special features are highly targeted tools that can reinforce serendipitous searching skills and lead users to specific, needed information quickly.

RE-ENVISIONING CLASSROOM INSTRUCTION

The ACRL Information Literacy Competency Standards for Higher Education prescribe the formulation of relevant searches as a fundamental concept of information literacy (*Information Literacy Competency*

Standards for Higher Education 2000). These standards encourage teaching keyword and Boolean search techniques so that the user can transfer these skills regardless of the resource. This technique largely reflects a traditional and "library-centric" approach, but is not always an intuitive way for users to search, and commonly ignores the refinements of many electronic resources to clarify needs and facilitate searching. In other words, the attempt to teach generic tools that reach across all electronic resources may downplay unique features in resources, such as the "more like this" option, that are particularly relevant to users. Unfortunately, information literacy instruction at the undergraduate level may never get past the simplistic notion of database "sameness."

This general approach, recommended by ACRL, is quite successful for research meant only to "dip one's toe" into the scientific literature, but is not sufficient for upper-division undergraduates faced with projects or assignments in their majors requiring far more comprehensive study. Fjallbrant and Levy explain that "subject-specific information literacy has additional dimensions and is closely related to the pattern of information flow within that discipline" (Fjallbrant and Levy 1999). As science and engineering students advance, they need to recognize both the many channels available for information in their disciplines and the many different searching mechanisms within these channels. Subject-specific information competency requires facility with a myriad of both print and electronic resources (e.g., handbooks and indexes) that provide comprehensive access to the literature needed for advanced study or research in science and engineering.

While electronic resources are very convenient for users, print resources must not be forgotten in subject-specific instruction. A recent Harvard survey reveals that the highest percentage of library resources used across disciplines are in print format. While they did not rate as highly as electronic on convenience, they were rated as superior in providing information needed by students, usefulness of material, reliability, and availability of assistance (Waters 2001).

Along with the continued need for print resources, specialized electronic resources continue to grow in importance. Powerful, sophisticated electronic resources (e.g., INSPEC, BIOSIS, SciFinder, and METADEX) provide unprecedented multiple-point access to a vast array of information. Yet, differences in citation/abstracting levels, lack of consistent search interfaces and results displays, and resource-unique controlled vocabulary often necessitate individualized training for effective use. According to Kutner, this lack of standardization "creates confusion for users when a wisely conducted search in one database is not interpreted the same way in another database" (Kutner 2000). This exemplifies a weakness of information literacy instruction that stresses similarities between resources yet fails to address the complexities of specialized electronic resources.

In order to gain the confidence and ability to successfully navigate information searches, students need both to see and to try the unique "bells & whistles" available, preferably at the time in their information pursuit when these options add value to their quest. Given the pragmatic nature of science and engineering students, timing of this resource-specific instruction to an assignment in hand is far more effective than "just-in-case" instruction that touts general search skills without a context in which to use them.

CONCLUSION

In order to impart the information literacy skills that will benefit students as science and engineering undergraduates and as they encounter information needs throughout their careers, librarians must remain aware of several issues:

- Science and engineering students differ from their peers in their academic activities and in the expectations of their instructors.
- Science and engineering undergraduates have unique curricular needs that will require specialized and targeted instruction.
- Online tutorials have not been adequately assessed as a educational tool for this population.
- The reference desk provides an immediate and valuable opportunity for context-specific information literacy instruction that builds upon serendipitous searching skills.
- Classroom information literacy instruction for this population needs to go beyond basic instruction emphasizing similarities among resources to instruction that emphasizes more complex understanding and subject-specific resources in all formats.

As the vision of a digital library environment continues to evolve, both successful comprehensive searching and serendipitous discovery of information should become more commonplace. Edelson and Gordin's *supportive scientific visualization environment* aims to provide adaptive advances in interface and activities design, organization and selection of materials, and functional documentation to support non-expert users as they build the requisite information skills in a scientific or technical discipline (Edelson and Gordin 1996). The current crop of electronic databases continues to evolve as well, with the continued development of such value-added, user-supportive features as alternative search strategy suggestions; sophisticated, accurate exclusion of unwanted information; and more refined cross linking to other search and/or results platforms. These digital enhancements, many of which are already being utilized, will continue to evolve and provide improved user support. They will not, however, negate the need for context-specific, hands-on, personalized instruction that can facilitate optimal user employment of these resources. Perhaps the science fiction vision of fully interactive, intelligent computers and information systems—combined with holographic librarians who inquire as to the "nature of your information emergency"—will be the reality of the future, and will allow for truly self-sufficient users. The reality in 2001, however, is that science and engineering undergraduates still benefit from some degree of human intervention. By demonstrating to undergraduates that databases and other information resources are valuable, usable tools, librarians will have taken an important step in making students information literate for life.

REFERENCES

Ackerson, Linda G. 1996. Basing Reference Service on Scientific Communication: Toward a More Effective Model for Science Graduate Students. *RQ* 36 (2): 248-260.

American Chemical Society, Committee on Professional Training. 1999. *Undergraduate Professional Education in Chemistry: Guidelines and Evaluation Procedures*. American Chemical Society [cited 24 May 2001]. Available from <http://www.acs.org/education/cpt/guidelines_fal199.pdf>.

Brown, Cecelia M. 1999. Information Literacy of Physical Science Graduate Students in the Information Age. *College & Research Libraries* 60 (5): 426-438.

Connell, Tschera H., and Jennifer E. Tipple. 1999. Testing the Accuracy of Information on the World Wide Web Using the AltaVista Search Engine. *Reference and User Services Quarterly* 38 (4): 360-368.

Dewald, Nancy H. 1999. Transporting Good Library Instruction Practices into the Web Environment: An Analysis of Online Tutorials. *The Journal of Academic Librarianship* 25 (1): 26-32.

Edelson, Daniel C., and Douglas N. Gordin. 1996. *Adapting Digital Libraries for Learners: Accessibility vs. Availability*. D-Lib Magazine [cited 24 May 2001]. Available from <http://www.dlib.org/dlib/september96/nwu/09edelson.html>.

Fjallbrant, Nancy, and Philippa Levy. 1999. *Information Literacy Courses in Engineering and Science: The Design and Implementation of the DEDICATE Courses: Distance Education Information Courses with Access Through Networks,* October

14, 1999 [cited May 24 2001]. Available from <http://educate.lib.chalmers.se/ IATUL/proceedcontents/chanpap/fjall.html>.

Hativa, Nira, and Menucha Birenbaum. 2000. WHO PREFERS WHAT? Disciplinary Differences in Students' Preferred Approaches to Teaching and Learning Styles. *Research in Higher Education* 41 (2): 209-236.

Herring, Susan D. 2001. Faculty Acceptance of the World Wide Web for Student Research. *College & Research Libraries* 62 (3): 251-258.

Information Literacy Competency Standards for Higher Education 2000. Association of College and Research Libraries [cited 24 May 2001]. Available from <http://www.ala. org/acrl/ilcomstan.html>.

Kellogg, Alex P. 2001. Looking Inward, Freshmen Care Less About Politics and More About Money. *Chronicle of Higher Education* 47 (20): A47-A51.

Kutner, Laurie A. 2000. *Library Instruction in an Interdisciplinary Environmental Studies Program: Challenges, Opportunities, and Reflections.* Issues in Science and Technology Librarianship [cited 24 May 2001]. Available from <http://www.library. ucsb.edu/istl/00-fall/article2.html>.

Leckie, Gloria J., and Anne Fullerton. 1999. Information Literacy in Science and Engineering Undergraduate Education: Faculty Attitudes and Pedagogical Practices. *College & Research Libraries* 60 (1): 9-29.

Sax, L. J., A.W. Astin, W.S. Korn, and K.M. Mahoney. 1998. *The American Freshman: National Norms for Fall 1998.* Los Angeles: Higher Education Research Institute, UCLA Graduate School of Education and Information Studies.

Waters, Donald J. 2001. *The Metadata Harvesting Initiative of the Mellon Foundation.* ARL Bimonthly Report 217. [cited 18 September 2001]. Available from <http://www.arl.org/newsltr/217/waters.html>.

Electronic Reserves in the Science Library: Tips, Techniques, and User Perceptions

Tina E. Chrzastowski

SUMMARY. Electronic reserve programs ("e-reserves") have brought a new perspective to a very traditional library service. Reserve services hold materials for a certain population's use and circulate them for short periods of time. Not limited to academic environments, reserve services can be found in special libraries and public libraries, but are traditionally a function of academic libraries in support of classroom teaching. Because there is a heavy demand placed on a limited group of materials (the reason they were initially selected for reserve), stresses on the reserve collection are legion, and include high rates of vandalism and theft, followed by endless fines and billing. This notoriously difficult collection has now been effectively moved online in many institutions, offering users better access and eliminating, or at least redirecting, many of the collection management challenges. The technology involved is relatively inexpensive and easily mastered. Libraries offering e-reserves can sim-

Tina E. Chrzastowski, MLS, is Chemistry Librarian and Professor of Library Administration, University of Illinois at Urbana-Champaign, Urbana, IL.

The author would like to thank and acknowledge Beth Tarr, Chemistry Library graduate assistant, who has refined and improved the library's e-reserve program during 2000-2001; Mary Laskowski, Coordinator of Media Services, Cataloging and Reserves, UIUC Undergraduate Library, who authored the original e-reserves student survey; David Ward, Reference Coordinator, UIUC Undergraduate Library, who assisted with the web survey; and Dr. Jeff Moore, Professor of Chemistry, UIUC, who allowed his Chemistry 331 course to be surveyed and who actively promoted and improved the e-reserves program.

[Haworth co-indexing entry note]: "Electronic Reserves in the Science Library: Tips, Techniques, and User Perceptions." Chrzastowski, Tina E. Co-published simultaneously in *Science & Technology Libraries* (The Haworth Information Press, an imprint of The Haworth Press, Inc.) Vol. 20, No. 2/3, 2001, pp. 107-119; and: *Electronic Resources and Services in Sci-Tech Libraries* (ed: Mary C. Schlembach, and William H. Mischo) The Haworth Information Press, an imprint of The Haworth Press, Inc., 2001, pp. 107-119. Single or multiple copies of this article are available for a fee from The Haworth Document Delivery Service [1-800-HAWORTH, 9:00 a.m. - 5:00 p.m. (EST). E-mail address: getinfo@haworthpressinc.com].

107

ply move existing programs online, or expand the service by offering e-books, videos, and links to related sites. Tips and techniques for implementing an e-reserves service in a science library are presented, copyright issues are addressed, and use and perceptions of e-reserves at the UIUC Chemistry Library are examined. *[Article copies available for a fee from The Haworth Document Delivery Service: 1-800-HAWORTH. E-mail address: <getinfo@haworthpressinc.com> Website: <http://www.HaworthPress.com> © 2001 by The Haworth Press, Inc. All rights reserved.]*

KEYWORDS. Electronic reserves, chemistry

INTRODUCTION

At the University of Illinois at Urbana-Champaign (UIUC) Chemistry Library, e-reserves grew out of need. The endless challenges of providing research materials to very large chemistry courses, with hundreds of students and limited copies of tests and notes, inspired the library staff to seek a technological solution. Vandalism and theft dogged the collection, and reserve users were limited to a set number of available copies and bound by finite library hours.

The solution was a web site operating 24/7 that contained all non-monographic reserve class materials. The homegrown electronic reserve program that developed from that need in 1997 has expanded and matured to meet increased demand and benefit from improved technology. Use of e-reserves is easily measured by monitoring web site visits. In addition, users' experiences and expectations are now evaluated through user-surveys, directing our energies toward the improvements they desire.

PREVIOUS STUDIES

E-reserves is not a new service, just a new way to conduct an existing service. Many academic libraries have accomplished this "system upgrade," either by purchasing commercial software to manage e-reserves, or by developing homegrown programs. E-reserve projects were created and reported by Hiller and Hiller (1999), Graves (1998), Laskowski and Ward (2001), Reichardt (1999), and Whitson (2000). Although some variation exists in methodology and scale, all studies report success with implementation and satisfaction among staff, faculty and students. This is also the experience with the e-reserves program at the UIUC Chemistry Library.

User survey evaluations were also conducted by a number of the libraries implementing e-reserves. Reichardt (1999) surveyed two different groups of students and found the younger, full-time student group favored e-reserves while the older, part-time student group preferred traditional print reserves. Whitson (2000) found 41% of e-reserve users accessed readings from home only, on a campus (University of Washington at Bothell) catering to "returning, working and/or commuting students." Reichardt's study supports this notion, finding that "the large majority of this group accessed materials from outside the library." Laskowski and Ward (2001) again confirm this preference for remote access, finding, "students accessed electronic reserves from a variety of places, by far the most popular being from off campus." Survey results from the UIUC Chemistry Library e-reserves program found similar results, which are reported later in this article.

METHODOLOGY, EQUIPMENT AND SOFTWARE

Since members of the library staff were in a problem-solving frame of mind, we looked for the simplest method for creating an e-reserves web site. Our Hewlett Packard (HP) scanner (ScanJet 6300C) came with HP software (HP DeskScan II) to create PDF (portable document format) documents. We use Adobe Acrobat Distiller version 3.01 for Windows to save EPS (scanned image files) files as PDF files. Adobe Acrobat Exchange is used to edit the PDF files, and Microsoft FrontPage 98 or Microsoft Notepad is used to edit the HTML (hyper text markup language) files. HTML is used to mount the documents on the web. Hardware used includes the scanner, a computer, and needed cables.

Adobe Acrobat Reader (freeware available at: http://www.adobe.com/products/acrobat/) is loaded on every public access terminal in the UIUC libraries, and our e-reserves web site links to this freeware for users to download (if needed) wherever they access the e-reserves site. These simple choices for equipment and software are typical of most e-reserve programs. In addition, server space is needed to host the web site. Very basic computer skills round out the requirement for setting up an e-reserves site.

Trial and error became the best instructor as we initiated the move to e-reserves. Although we were novice web site managers, very few mistakes were made. One early error was creating individual files for each scanned page, rather than linking each page in document groupings. This decision was made in 1997, when loading large files (such as a many-paged course review) took much longer to display than with today's technology. This file organization was altered when network speeds caught up with file size display. Now users are prompted to view an entire document, with the number of pages in the document noted for reference. A second glitch came when users needed to access the web site from a non-campus computer. This problem initiated the proxy server access and authentication, which now allows any valid UIUC student, staff or faculty to use their net ID to authenticate themselves and gain access to the site.

While the pdf format is the most common format used on the site, also supported are .jpg and .mov, which are used, for example, for displaying movies of moving molecules. These formats require the plug-in Chime, free chemical structure visualization software available from Molecular Design Limited (MDL) (http://www.mdlchime.com/chime/). MDL requires registration for use, but once registered with MDL, Chime can be downloaded and used to view these e-reserves. When different (especially non-text) formats are used in e-reserves, easily downloadable freeware must be readily available at the site, with clear instructions for use.

Unlike the larger-scale e-reserves program at the UIUC Undergraduate Library (Laskowski and Ward, 2001), the Chemistry Library e-reserves site is not integrated into the Library's online catalog with records in the "Reserve Room" electronic catalog. Instead, a web site listing each chemistry course with electronic reserves is created each semester and linked off the Chemistry Library homepage. It is also linked from class web pages, when they exist. As with print reserves, materials are removed from reserves at the end of each semester. Files that contain non-copyrighted material are stored off-line for possible use in future semesters. Figure 1 shows a screen shot of the e-reserves home page for the UIUC Chemistry Library site for fall semester 2001. Links are created from the homepage to each class and within each class to material submitted by the instructor.

The library personnel primarily responsible for the scanning of reserve materials and maintaining the web site are the Chemistry Library graduate assistants, who work weekday evenings and weekends. Our goal is to keep e-reserves current. Materials are promised to be posted within 24 hours of receipt, and are usually online within just a few hours. We accept submissions in print (for scanning) or electronic format (disk, email or ftp).

FIGURE 1. Screen Shot of UIUC Chemistry Library Course Reserve Homepage: http://www.library.uiuc.edu/chx/reserves/

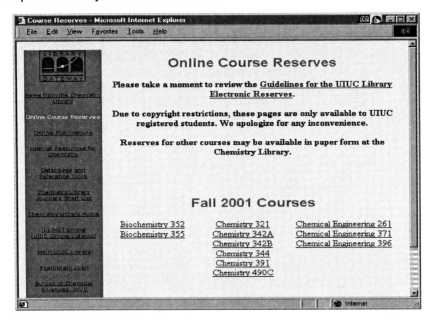

COPYRIGHT

While the majority of items currently on e-reserve at the UIUC Chemistry Library are not copyrighted (notes, tests, exams, homework, web links, video), copyrighted materials are posted with proper acknowledgment and fees are paid, if required. Laskowski and Ward (2001) describe the process the UIUC Library used to develop an e-reserves copyright policy, including clearance by the University's legal office and approval by the Library's Administrative Council. The policy equates ownership of print and digital versions for fair educational use, citing Section 107 of the United States Copyright Act of 1976. The full policy is linked from every UIUC e-reserves site and is found online at: http://www.library. uiuc.edu/geninfo/electronicreserves.htm.

Site access is limited only to UIUC users through IP (Internet Protocol) checking; users can also use their net ID to authenticate themselves as UIUC students, staff or faculty to access restricted web pages from non-campus IP addresses. In addition to this restriction, the only link to copyrighted articles is through class number. No index or link by author's name or the title of the article is made available. In addition, reserve files are taken off the server at the end of each semester.

Copyright is a critical issue in print and electronic reserve services. Many articles have addressed and interpreted reserve copyright policy, resulting in differing viewpoints and conclusions. Four fairly recent articles that address copyright in the electronic reserve environment are Crews (1999), Graves (2000), Loring (1997), and Melamut (2000). Each library environment must address the copyright issue and meet the requirements set by the governing body supervising the library before an effective e-reserves service can be mounted. This is not a step that can be addressed later or thought about as you go, unless the e-reserves program is limited to non-copyrighted material only.

PROGRAM EVALUATION

As with any new service, evaluation is critical to future success. Until 2001, student and faculty voluntary feedback was our primary evaluation tool. Following the successful survey sponsored by the UIUC Undergraduate Library (Laskowski and Ward, 2001), a similar survey was initiated for students in Chemistry 331, "Elementary Organic Chemistry II," an organic chemistry course for upper level undergraduates that strongly encouraged use of e-reserves. In fact, no print reserve material was available for this class; reserves for Chemistry 331 were available exclusively online.

A web survey was created based on the one conducted by the UIUC Undergraduate Library. All 146 students in Chemistry 331 were asked to take the survey, answering questions about their experience with e-reserves. Results from the survey were mostly positive, and not surprising. Out of 146 students in the class (and 146 respondents), 90% said they used e-reserves sometime during the course. When asked where they accessed e-reserves, 84 (57%) named "from a computer at home" as the most popular site, confirming findings from previous research. This was followed by campus computing sites (56 or 38%), the Undergraduate Library (28 or 19%), residence hall computer (24 or 16%), and campus libraries other than Undergraduate or Chemistry (20 or 14%). Other places cited were "lab, friends, fraternity houses, and 'at work.'" Respondents were encouraged to check as many places as they used.

Questions were asked concerning the students' preference for reading reserves in print or online. When asked their access choice, 41 (28%) said they read reserves online only, 23 (16%) said they printed out the materials from the web site (no print counterpart was made available), and 67 (46%) said they did some of both.

To find out how format might affect use of materials, the question was asked, "Does the ability to access reserve materials online change the amount of reserve material you are willing to read?" The options for answers were "I read more, I read the same as always, and, I read less." Table 1 shows the response from the students. The majority said they read as much or more reserve material as they did with traditional print materials.

To truly serve as an evaluation tool, students were asked what they liked best and least about electronic reserves. Table 2 shows that the positives are truly positive, while the negatives shown in Table 3, such as "poor download time from home" and "more material needs to be available online" are things that are either going to be resolved with technology, or that could be part of an expanding e-reserves program. In addition, the second-most cited complaint, "should be linked directly from library homepage," is already a fact–all course reserves are linked directly from the Chemistry Library homepage. It's possible that many students felt they should not have to go from the homepage to the reserves page to their course page.

Finally, the last question asked was, "After using electronic reserves, which do you prefer, traditional or electronic reserves?" Table 4 outlines the replies, showing 101 students (69%) preferred e-reserves to traditional print reserves, with a comparatively big drop in the number of students preferring print (14, or 10%). As with most of the electronic reserves projects reported in the literature, this program proved to be an effective way to improve reserve service and make users happy.

Much simpler than a survey, another type of e-reserves evaluation is monitoring use of the service. Web servers are easily set up to measure the number of hits a site receives. We can measure use by course, as well as focus on specific pages that are viewed. Table 5 shows use statistics for Chemistry 331 for each week the course was in session. The professor for this course specifically asked for these data in order to gauge the use of

TABLE 1. Responses to the Question, "Does the Ability to Access Reserve Materials Online Change the Amount of Reserve Material You Are Willing to Read?"

Amount read	Read more	Read the same amount	Read less
# Respondents (146)	63	71	11
Percentage	43%	49%	8%

TABLE 2. Responses to the Question, "What Did You Like Best About Electronic Reserves? Please Check All That Apply."

Reason	No need to go to library	Availability throughout semester	Printing them out	Ease/ speed of access	No need to wait at Reserve Desk	No need to purchase course pack	Other	No Response
Number of Respondents (146)	109	100	94	83	83	37	5	3
Percentage*	75%	68%	64%	57%	57%	25%	3%	2%

*Respondents could select multiple answers, so the total percentage is greater than 100.

TABLE 3. Responses to the Question, "What Did You Like Least About Electronic Reserves? Please Check All That Apply."

Reason	Download time or access from home	Should be linked directly from library homepage	More material needs to be available online	Poor image resolution	Difficult to logon	System down time	Materials not in a clear order	Other*	No response
Number of Respondents (146)	55	53	42	39	20	18	9	13	2
Percentage*	38%	36%	29%	27%	17%	12%	6%	9%	1%

*Respondents could select multiple answers, so the total percentage is greater than 100.

114

TABLE 4. Responses to the Question, "After Using Electronic Reserves, Which Do You Prefer, Traditional or Electronic Reserves?"

Access Preference	Electronic	Traditional	No Preference	Did Not Use Electronic Reserves
# Respondents (146)	101	14	23	7
Percentage	69%	10%	16%	5%

TABLE 5. Weekly Use Statistics for Chemistry 331 E-Reserves Web Sites for Spring Semester 2001. A "Use" Is Counted Each Time a Web Page Is Viewed.

Date	Chemistry 331 Electronic Reserves
1/13/01-1/19/01	693
1/20/01-1/27/01	1542
1/28/01-2/3/01	2273
2/4/01-2/10/01	3863
2/11/01-2/17/01	5628
2/18/01-2/24/01	1935
2/25/01-3/3/01	1610
3/4/01-3/10/01	2110
3/11/01-3/17/01	550
3/18/01-3/24/01	5001
3/25/01-3/31/01	1893
4/1/01-4/7/01	1304
4/8/01-4/14/01	1431
4/15/01-4/21/01	1787
4/22/01-4/28/01	3330
4/29/01-5/5/01	5478
5/6/01-5/12/01	1183

his time in preparing materials for the site. Use is fairly steady throughout the semester, peaking around midterms (March 18-24) and finals (May 29-April 5), and dropping dramatically during spring break week (March 11-17). These use patterns are familiar to any reserve clerk, but the volume is many times higher than we were observing with print reserves. This high use may be recording the many multiple viewings that users make when relying solely on an online copy. The survey found that 28% of users were not making print copies from the e-reserves files, indicating that repeated online viewing of the same materials was probably taking the place of printing. The total use of the Chemistry 331 site was 41,611 uses in spring semester. With 146 students, this averages to about 285 web page viewings per person. The total use of all chemistry library reserve pages for spring semester 2001 was 114,486 "hits."

In order to obtain the best results in surveying users about electronic reserve use, the following recommendations are made:

> Work with faculty to initiate feedback within the class setting.
> *Students take the survey more seriously if members of the faculty are involved.*
>
> Give credit for taking the survey.
> *Our survey was worth one quiz grade in Chemistry 331.*
>
> As with any survey, keep it simple and replicable.
> *Our survey was based directly on the e-reserve survey in the Undergraduate Library, with specific questions added for chemistry library users.*
>
> Do it ONLINE, but offer paper backup.
> *The goal is to move users from paper to online. While an online survey is preferred, offer a back up paper survey for those who simply have not yet made the shift to online.*

TIPS AND TECHNIQUES

Based on the experiences with e-reserves over the past four years, and the survey responses from chemistry students, a few lessons have been learned.

Listen to Users

What are the problems and how can they be resolved? User concerns about access to e-reserves from non-UIUC IP addresses led directly to creating a proxy server for authentication. Also, an email address to report problems and complaints is essential, and must be read and replied to daily. These are the problems your users care enough about to contact you, not waiting to be asked what they think. Read, solve, and reply!

Focus on Dependability

Dependability is the most important factor. The web site must always be accessible–ALWAYS. The site exists to be 24/7. Expect many complaints if this service level is not reached.

Put All the Rules Up Front

The copyright policy, any needed software, and access issues such as proxy information and limits to UIUC users only, need to be first on the web site.

Prepare for Your Environment to Change

Change breeds more change: an e-reserve program can mean reduced circulation, reduced photocopier statistics (and revenue), and a shift from in-person to email reference questions. The environment supporting the old model of print reserves will change. Be prepared to answer questions about why the library's workflow and use patterns are shifting. Bring the staff along. Offer training, talk about how jobs will shift with a move to electronic reserves, and ask staff to monitor user responses. Front-line staff know a great deal about what users want.

Keep Statistics

ALWAYS keep statistics, especially if you have management data pre-implementation for comparison. Think about what statistics you'll need. Will the server check use? Whose responsibility will it be to query the server about use? How often do you want to collect these data?

Equipment

Scanners are coming down in price. Buy the best you can afford. A best bet is a scanner with automatic paper feeder. Make sure your printers can handle the quality needed for reserve material. The UIUC Library charges for copies, but they are good quality laser printers. We also know from the survey and statistics that e-reserve users are not reliant on chemistry library printers, preferring, we believe, to either not print or to print at a free site (at home, at work, at friends).

Just Do It

Don't wait for your parent organization to begin an e-reserve program. If you are interested, just do it (following that copyright policy check). This is easy! And electronic reserves support the role your library plays as a subject-specific, special library, that of strong departmental support filling the special needs of its clientele.

Push the Envelope

Once you've set up your e-reserves program, find out what your clientele are doing with it, and what they want to do with it. You may be adding e-books, video, audio or moving molecules. Add software as necessary (such as Chime for chemical structures). Make sure software is licensed or free, and has easy downloading capabilities.

WHAT'S NEXT?

The e-reserves program at the UIUC Chemistry Library looks forward to growth and change. We've only just begun to find ways to provide quick, convenient, remote access for our clientele. A few of the next steps we're considering include requiring participation in e-reserves and therefore eliminating any print materials (except monographs), adding e-books and e-texts for the courses, and supporting remote users by continuing to investigate improved technology. We also plan to promote the library as *the* source for classroom e-reserves, or in turn, support links to class sites to keep the library in this game. And we will continue to conduct user surveys to gather patron feedback.

CONCLUSION

Successfully establishing and maintaining an electronic reserves program is not difficult. The effort and the equipment involved are well within most libraries' means. As computer dependence continues to grow, demand for remotely accessed library materials grows, and will include reserve material. It is important to continue to support reserves as a library service. If libraries do not enter into this arena, professors, teaching assistants and secretaries will be creating class web sites, effectively moving reserves from a library to a classroom service.

The challenge is to continue to be responsive and support this service within our resource and technology limits. As we have found over the past few years, faculty and student interest and use of e-reserves materials drives the program. Being responsive to patrons is the library's goal, and by shifting resources and employing readily available technology we are able to meet that goal.

REFERENCES

Crews, Kenneth D. 1999. "Electronic reserves and fair use: the outer limits of CONFU." *Journal of the American Society for Information Science* 50(14): 1342-1345.

Graves, Karen J. 2000. "Electronic reserves: copyright and permissions." *Bulletin of the Medical Library Association* 88 (1): 18-25.

Graves, Karen J. 1998. "Re-engineering the library for improved access to electronic health information: electronic reserves." *Libri* 48: 237-241.

Hiller, Bud and Hiller, Tammy Bunn. 1999. "Electronic reserves and success: where do you stop?" *Journal of Interlibrary Loan, Document Delivery & Information Supply* 10 (2): 61-75.

Laskowski, Mary S. and Ward, David H. 2001. "Creation and management of a home-grown electronic reserves system at an academic library: results from a pilot project. *Journal of Academic Librarianship*. In press.

Loring, Christopher B. 1997. "Library reserves and copyright: thirty years on and still changing." *Library Acquisitions: Practice and Theory* 21 (1): 29-39.

Melamut, Steven J. 2000. "Pursuing fair use, law libraries, and electronic reserves." *Law Library Journal* 92 (2): 157-192.

Reichardt, Karen. 1999. "Electronic reserves at a small college library: from research to reality." *Technical Services Quarterly* 17 (1): 1-12.

Whitson, Katherine A. 2000. "Electronic Reserves–Pilot and Evaluation." *Journal of Interlibrary Loan, Document Delivery & Information Supply* 10 (3): 29-41.

Trends in Current Awareness Services

Mary C. Schlembach

SUMMARY. Current Awareness Services such as Table of Contents (TOC) or Selected Dissemination of Information (SDI) have been a mainstay in science and engineering libraries for many years. With the proliferation of Web-based full-text journals and the availability of e-resource registries and sophisticated integrated library systems, the process of providing current awareness services with access to full-text have been re-emphasized and re-shaped. This paper will describe current awareness services implemented in the Grainger Engineering Library Information Center at the University of Illinois at Urbana-Champaign. These services include: e-mail notices of current journal Table of Contents with links to available full-text; access to a Web-based currently received journal list with links to TOC of issues and full-text; custom e-mail notices of newly received books. University of Illinois College of Engineering faculty have greatly benefited from these TOC services in their research and teaching. Their input has helped librarians to develop more efficient services that best meet their needs. *[Article copies available for a fee from The Haworth Document Delivery Service: 1-800-HAWORTH. E-mail address: <getinfo@haworthpressinc.com> Website: <http://www.HaworthPress.com> © 2001 by The Haworth Press, Inc. All rights reserved.]*

KEYWORDS. Current awareness service, table of contents, selected dissemination of information, engineering, electronic services

Mary C. Schlembach, MLS, Certificate of Advanced Studies in Library Automation, is Assistant Engineering Librarian for Digital Services, University of Illinois at Urbana-Champaign, Urbana, IL.

[Haworth co-indexing entry note]: "Trends in Current Awareness Services." Schlembach, Mary C. Co-published simultaneously in *Science & Technology Libraries* (The Haworth Information Press, an imprint of The Haworth Press, Inc.) Vol. 20, No. 2/3, 2001, pp. 121-132; and: *Electronic Resources and Services in Sci-Tech Libraries* (ed: Mary C. Schlembach and William H. Mischo) The Haworth Information Press, an imprint of The Haworth Press, Inc., 2001, pp. 121-132. Single or multiple copies of this article are available for a fee from The Haworth Document Delivery Service [1-800-HAWORTH, 9:00 a.m. - 5:00 p.m. (EST). E-mail address: getinfo@haworthpressinc.com].

BACKGROUND

Current Awareness Services such as Table of Contents (TOC) or Selected Dissemination of Information (SDI) have been a mainstay in science and engineering libraries for many years. Over the past decade academic and corporate libraries have provided selected dissemination of information (SDI) to educators and researchers as part of their basic services (Allen 1994). Traditional current awareness services have centered on notifying library patrons when new journal issues have been published or received by the library. Historically, libraries would distribute photocopied paper copies of the Tables of Contents of specific journal titles to patrons that requested those titles or post copies in a common area for review. It was the responsibility of the patron to follow-up by retrieving a copy of articles relevant to their research.

THE SWITCH TO ELECTRONIC CURRENT AWARENESS SERVICES

With the introduction of serial check-in systems and with journal issue alerting services, libraries started to send journal tables of contents to their patrons through electronic means. At the same time online database vendors, such as Dialog, Ovid, BRS, and CARL UnCover introduced SDI services for users (Rowley 1994). These services allowed users to store a profile of journal names and keywords for typically a monthly online alerting notification service. These two trends allowed libraries to build "profiles" of journal titles and relay the Table of Contents electronically to each patron. This greatly improved current awareness services. As Llull noted in 1991, "Using electronic communications over campus networks to perform library functions is not only efficient but also works to penetrate the physical and organizational barriers of being in different buildings and being members of different departments" (Llull 1991).

Providing e-mail-based electronic current awareness services gave libraries the ability to switch from a "pull" service to a "push" service for their patrons. A "pull" service responds to user needs by matching particular requests with the items in the database. A "push" service, on the other hand, proactively alerts users to new items added to an information resource database (Tedd and Yeates 1998).

In the last few years libraries have moved to a Web-based environment for their information retrieval services. The current trend is to develop custom library portals that utilize e-resource registries which include detailed information about and links to full-text electronic journals (Lakos and Gray 2000). The advent of these e-resource registries has introduced an entirely new aspect to current awareness services (Jordan 2000, Morgan and Reade 2000). Libraries now can deliver or push links to full-text journals and articles within journals as part of their current awareness services. Providing these full-text links is one of the most important trends in current awareness services. The ability to provide links to the full-text of the cited article is considered by users to be one of the most valuable features of electronic journals (Liew 2000, Hurd 2001).

This paper will describe three electronic current awareness services implemented in the Grainger Engineering Library Information Center at the University of Illinois at Urbana-Champaign (UIUC). These services integrate e-resource registries, custom local databases, vendor database services, and the online catalog. These three services are:

- An e-mail based current journal Table of Contents service that provides links to available full-text;
- Access to a Web-based currently received journal list with links to TOC of specific issues and full-text;
- Custom e-mail notices of newly received books.

CURRENT JOURNAL TOCS WITH LINKS TO AVAILABLE FULL-TEXT

In 1995, the Grainger Engineering Library staff wrote a Table of Contents program which searched for journal titles in the ISI Current Contents database using the native mode of BRS (Bibliographic Record Service).

In 1998, the University of Illinois Library switched from the BRS system to Ovid. Ovid offers a SDI capability that allows patrons to save search strategies and execute searches on a monthly basis against database updates. Initially this service was not activated in our local Ovid system. Later, because of our ability to add the local call numbers and locations to the journal Table of Contents display, we decided not to utilize the Ovid SDI capability for our journal current awareness service. Currently we are also able to add full-text links, when available, to the current awareness e-mail notifications.

BRS native mode is offered within the Ovid interface. The software that Grainger staff had written for the BRS system was adaptable to the Ovid system with only a few changes. The Grainger TOC service utilizes a relational Microsoft Access database with three tables: faculty, journals, and toc. The faculty table lists all participating faculty and includes name, address, phone, e-mail address, and a unique id field (facid). The journals table includes fields such as title, ISSN, call number, an e-resource id number (onlineid) that provides the hypertext link to the full-text, and a different unique id number (jrnid). The toc table is the "pivot" between the other two tables and contains two fields: the faculty table id (facid) and the journal id (jrnid). The id fields in the faculty and journal tables are set to a one-to-many relationship in the toc table. Figure 1 displays the relationships between the three tables.

Figure 2 illustrates the relative simplicity of the Table of Contents program interface. The program connects to the Current Contents database, and the user simply clicks the Run TOC button. The Table of Contents program uses the individual faculty member id along with their e-mail address, the journal ISSN number and the toc table to search the Current Contents database, limiting the results to the last entry week. If there is a result, the program then sends the Table of Contents and the hypertext link to the full-text, if available, to the faculty member. Figure 3 is a sample of an e-mail sent to the faculty member with full-text link and Table of Contents with abstracts.

FIGURE 1

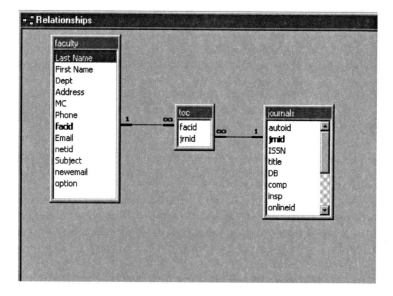

FIGURE 2

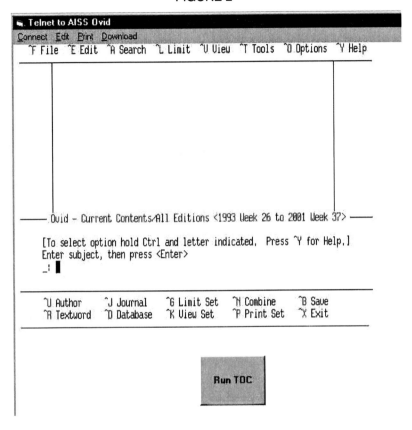

The full-text links provided in the bi-weekly TOC service have proven to be extremely popular and useful. Over 240 College of Engineering (COE) faculty members presently receive e-mail containing weekly tables of contents from a locally loaded Ovid Current Contents database. The e-mailed Table of Contents are generated from a faculty member's custom search profile in which they indicate the specific journals and subject areas of interest to them. Research has show that users appreciate current awareness services that integrate in-house data or profiles and external information (Rowley 1994). In a survey of COE faculty receiving the Table of Contents service, 96% indicated that the full-text links were "Important" or "Very Important."

FIGURE 3

An electronic full-text version of this journal is available to UIUC faculty/students/staff at:

http://www.library.uiuc.edu/eresource/get.asp?rid=1076

```
<1>
Authors
 Brokman A.  King AH.  Vilenkin AJ.
Title
 The role of segregation in diffusion-induced grain boundary
 migration
Source
 Acta Materialia. 49(1):1-11, 2001 Jan 8.
Abstract
 The problem of grain boundary motion in the diffusion field
 of a solute is formulated for the case of infinitely fast
 diffusion along a straight boundary. The steady state
 solution suggests that (de)alloying occurs by two different
 modes, namely: the solute diffusion through the stationary
 boundary to the bulk, or by diffusion-induced grain
 boundary migration (DIGM). The transition from one mode to
 another depends on the grain boundary segregation
 coefficient. The result enables an assessment of the
 relative importance of different possible driving forces.
 When the equilibrium concentrations of the bulk solute with
 the external gas is low, the entropy of mixing is the
 leading driving force. DIGM does not occur in isotope
 solution because the solute atom does not segregate to the
 boundary. Based on this theory, we construct the phase
 diagram in the plane of the (gas/bulk) equilibrium
 concentration vs the segregation coefficient, representing
 the transition from DIGM to alloying via stationary
 boundaries. (C) 2001 Acta Materialia Inc. Published by
 Elsevier Science Ltd. All rights reserved. [References: 11]
Institution
 Reprint available from:
```

In addition to the journal Table of Contents being sent to researchers we are planning to expand faculty profiles to include subject keywords and/or descriptor terms to provide an even more inclusive current awareness service. Faculty and researchers in many disciplines require a constant flow of current and often highly specialized information. An innovative library response is to develop ongoing individualized information services (Butler 1993).

CURRENTLY RECEIVED JOURNAL LIST WITH LINKS TO TOC OF ISSUES AND FULL-TEXT

The College of Engineering at UIUC has approximately 400 faculty members and nearly 4,000 graduate-level students. Currently the Table of Contents service is restricted to COE faculty and post-doctoral researchers. Due to the large number and the inconsistency of their presence on campus, we do not provide current awareness services for graduate students.

For graduate students and faculty who do not want to receive the Table of Contents as a regular service, we provide access to Web-based journal lists that link to a title's Table of Contents and the full-text, when available. The Grainger Library Web page has several custom designed databases that provide specific information about engineering and science-related materials. The "Currently Received Journals" database integrates print journal check-in information with links to available full-text and specific issue tables of contents displays. The current journal display shown in Figure 4 shows the links to full-text and tables of contents. The Table of Contents display is dynamically extracted from the Current Contents database via a search by ISSN, volume number, and issue number. The Web site uses custom dynamic link library (.dll) software written by Grainger staff that connects to the Current Contents database running under Ovid. The software extracts the Table of Contents information and presents the display to the user within the Currently Received Journals Web site (Mischo and Schlembach 1999).

FIGURE 4

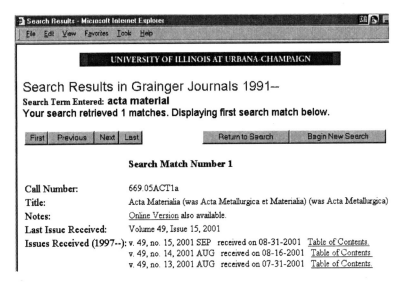

Providing expanded access to full-text journals and conference series from within different contexts is an important service challenge. At the Grainger Library, availability and link information for approximately 700 engineering related full text journals is maintained in a custom database. This e-journals database is used to provide links to full-text journals within the Grainger Table of Contents (TOC) service, the Grainger Journals database, and several custom databases that provide holdings of the ACM and IEEE publications. See the Chan article in this volume for detailed information on the e-resource registry application (Chan 2001).

NEWLY RECEIVED BOOKS

Ideal current awareness services should alert users to all items of interest, which means a very wide coverage extending beyond journals to other literature such as conferences and reports (Mountifield 1995). For this reason, we have extended the Table of Contents service to include New Books. This service also employs a Visual Basic program that utilizes custom local databases to extract information on faculty research interests and the subject areas of new books. The two custom databases are the Engineering Faculty database and the New Books database, both maintained by Grainger Library staff.

The Engineering Faculty database contains records for all current, emeritus, and former University of Illinois College of Engineering faculty. It includes their College department, e-mail address, links to their personal Web page, place and date of degrees, awards and milestones, and primary research interests. Figure 5 presents a record from the Engineering Faculty database.

The New Books database was originally started in 1998 in order to track books being received by the Grainger Library (one of 42 departmental libraries) and provide a simple way to browse new books for library patrons. New Books are shelved in a special area of the library and circulate for a shorter time period. Fields included in the new books database includes title, author/editors, ISBN, date received, call number, series title, publisher, year published, and subjects. These fields are extracted from the DRA online catalog by custom macros that allow a library staff member to scan the barcode and extract the appropriate MARC-coded information (Bregman and Chan 2001).

The New Books current awareness service is run once a month. It parses each subject field from the New Books database and compares them to the Interests field of the Engineering Faculty database (see Figure 6).

FIGURE 5

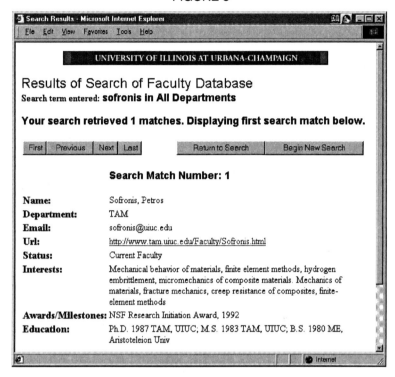

Each subject heading is parsed into its constituent words and run separately. Each subject heading is run separately in situations where a single title has multiple subject headings. A few subject terms are removed due to the broadness in definition (i.e., systems, materials, techniques, and congresses). Other subject terms are modified to make them more appropriate for searching. For example, the subject term "robotics" was truncated to the term "robot," since we had no matches with "robotics" but had several matches with "robot." The lack of LC Subject headings in the Faculty Interest database is partially compensated for by the breakup of subject headings into component words.

Only current faculty members are notified about new titles. The results for each title are checked to remove duplication of faculty names. The program then sends an e-mail with title, call number, and location information to the faculty member notifying them of all new titles received in the last month that are relevant to their interests. Presently there are 25

FIGURE 6

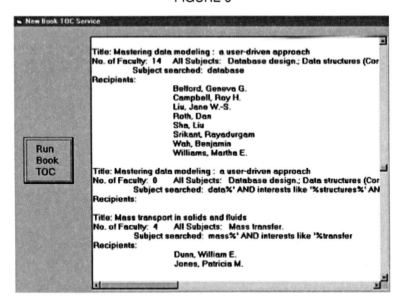

faculty participating in a pilot study of this service. For faculty who do not wish to receive regular email notification, we also link lists of new books to the faculty members' records within the Faculty Interest database. This feature also assists the graduate students of a faculty member by helping them review new resources in their subject area(s).

CONCLUSION

There are clear benefits to providing varied types of current awareness services for science and technology researchers. These current awareness systems demonstrate the power and service capability of "push" technologies. As libraries deliver more services to users outside the library building, it is clear that providing full-text links will become increasingly important. Also any assistance that researchers receive from the library creates better relations when faculty need to be called upon to support library budgets. Additionally, librarians can better understand the research interests of their constituents by becoming familiar with the subject areas in which each faculty member is working. Another benefit to librarians is that information gathered in the initial and ongoing profiling activities can be applied to their collection development planning (Butler 1993).

Cox and Hanson pointed out that an electronic current awareness service designed to appeal to busy researchers in academic and research organizations will:

- be administered by the library
- deliver search results from major bibliographic databases
- offer search profiles designed for individual researchers' specific information needs
- offer weekly or monthly intervals
- deliver results that can be imported into a personal database (Cox and Hanson 1992).

The services offered by the Grainger Engineering Library meet these criteria. In addition, faculty members can request document delivery services from any of the Grainger current awareness services to assist their research.

REFERENCES

Allen, Robert S. 1994. Current Awareness Service for Special Libraries Using Microcomputer Based *Current Contents on Diskette. Special Libraries* 85 (Winter):35-43.

Bregman, Alvan and Chan, Winnie S. 2001. Customization of Library Service in a Cross-Platform Programming Environment. *Information Technology and Libraries* 20(1):21-28.

Butler, John T. 1993. A Current Awareness Service Using Microcomputer Databases and Electronic Mail. *College & Research Libraries* 54 (March):115-123.

Chan, Winnie. 2001. Creative Applications of a Web-Based E-Resource Registry. *Science & Technology Libraries* 20(2/3):45-56.

Cox, John and Hanson, Terry. 1992. Setting up an Electronic Current Awareness Service. *Online* 16 (July):36-43.

Hurd, Julie M. Digital Collections: Acceptance and Use in a Research Community. *Crossing the Divide: Proceedings of Tenth ACRL National Conference*, March 25-16, 2001, Denver, CO, p. 312-319 <http://www.ala.org/acrl/papers01/hurd.pdf> (accessed August 28, 2001).

Jordan, William. 2000. My Gateway at the University of Washington Libraries *Information Technology and Libraries* 19(4):180-185.

Liew, Chern Li.; Foo, Schubert.; Chennupati, K. R. 2000. A Study of Graduate Student End-Users' Use and Perception of Electronic Journals. *Online Information Review* 24(4):302-315.

Llull, Harry. 1991. Meeting the Academic and Research Information Needs of Scientists and Engineers in the University Environment. *Science & Technology Libraries* 11 (Spring):83-90.

Mischo, William H. and Schlembach, Mary C. 1999. Web-based Access to Locally Developed Databases. *Library Computing* 18(1):51-58.

Morgan, Keith and Reade, Tripp. 2000. Pioneering Portals: MyLibrary@NCState. *Information Technology and Libraries* 19(4):191-198.

Mountlfield, H.M. 1995. Electronic current awareness service: a survival tool for the information age? *The Electronic Library* 13(4):317-324.

Pinelli, Thomas E. 1991. The information-seeking habits and practices of engineers. *Science & Technology Libraries* 11:5-25.

Rowley, Jennifer. 1994. Revolution in current awareness services. *Journal of Librarianship and Information Science* 26(1):7-14.

Tedd, Lucy A. and Yeates, Robin. 1998. A personalised current awareness service for library and information services staff: an overview of the NewsAgent for Libraries project. *Program* 32(4):373-390.

Library Portals, Simultaneous Search, and Full-Text Linking Technologies

William H. Mischo

SUMMARY. Libraries are engaged in the development of customized portals or information gateways designed to reduce information overload and provide enhanced access to distributed information resources. Among the concerns that are being addressed in the next generation of library portals are: (1) providing enhanced navigation and linking through the rapidly growing number of electronic resources, in particular full-text resources; and (2) providing the capability of searching multiple information resources–such as periodical index databases, the library online catalog, and Web search engines–from a single user interface form. The technologies that will provide linking between discrete full-text resources and from periodical index databases and online catalogs to full-text will become increasingly important. These linking technologies are being built around information standards such as the Digital Object Identifier (DOI) and the CrossRef publishers' initiative. Libraries are also building e-resource registry databases that identify and provide links to available licensed electronic full-text resources.

This paper will describe the role of portal services and examine the technologies involved in full-text linking. The paper will also describe a portal application that was developed at the Grainger Engineering Library Information Center at the University of Illinois at Urbana-Champaign (UIUC), which features simultaneous search and dynamic linking capabilities over multiple information resources. This simultaneous search service provides a model for synchronous searching of in-

William H. Mischo is Head, Grainger Engineering Library Information Center and Professor of Library Administration, University of Illinois at Urbana-Champaign, Urbana, IL.

[Haworth co-indexing entry note]: "Library Portals, Simultaneous Search, and Full-Text Linking Technologies." Mischo, William H. Co-published simultaneously in *Science & Technology Libraries* (The Haworth Information Press, an imprint of The Haworth Press, Inc.) Vol. 20, No. 2/3, 2001, pp. 133-147; and: *Electronic Resources and Services in Sci-Tech Libraries* (ed: Mary C. Schlembach, and William H. Mischo) The Haworth Information Press, an imprint of The Haworth Press, Inc., 2001, pp. 133-147. Single or multiple copies of this article are available for a fee from The Haworth Document Delivery Service [1-800-HAWORTH, 9:00 a.m. - 5:00 p.m. (EST). E-mail address: getinfo@haworthpressinc.com].

133

formation resources and offers full-text linking capabilities built around a custom UIUC e-resource database, the CrossRef metadata database, and the article DOI. *[Article copies available for a fee from The Haworth Document Delivery Service: 1-800-HAWORTH. E-mail address: <getinfo@haworthpressinc. com> Website: <http://www.HaworthPress.com> © 2001 by The Haworth Press, Inc. All rights reserved.]*

KEYWORDS. Portals, simultaneous searching, digital object identifiers, full-text, linking, CrossRef, Grainger Engineering Library

INTRODUCTION

Libraries have been actively involved in the development and deployment of customized portal and gateway sites designed to provide enhanced user access to information resources (Zemon 2001, Ketchell 2000). Indeed, this has been defined as a key role for libraries and librarians in the era of the user-centered, customized "digital library" (Deiss 1999, Campbell 2000, Guenther 2000, Lakos and Gray 2000).

At the same time, many publishers and commercial information providers are enhancing their full-text repository sites to provide portal services and links to the resources of other publishers and service providers. They are doing this through reciprocal linking arrangements with other publishers and by loading subject-discipline A & I service databases on their sites. These publisher "megasites" (such as Elsevier's ScienceDirect) provide search, browse, and linking capabilities over Elsevier full-text resources as well as links to other publisher repositories and discipline specific periodical index databases.

Library and vendor portal services provide users with integrated paths through remote and local content providers and other university and commercial portals. They attempt to bring together and integrate the disparate full-text publisher repositories, the secondary information resources and local finding tools/aids in order to provide users with a systematic "view" of the information landscape. Ketchell has noted, "customization, personalization, vertical integration, and sophisticated searching are approaches libraries are using to tame the portal glut" (Ketchell 2000).

Perhaps the two key foci of library, publisher, and vendor portals is tying together the twin initiatives of: (1) robust search/navigation, with (2) the ability to link everywhere from anywhere–including between discrete full-text articles and from A & I services and the online catalog to full-text.

There are a number of vendor and library systems in various stages of production or development that provide simultaneous search and retrieval over multiple data resources. It is quite clear that vendors view simultaneous search capabilities as a very important component in their overarching system architectures.

And, the ability to provide reference links–automatic links from the references in one paper to the referred-to article–is considered by users to be a valuable feature (Liew 2000, Hurd 2001) and the single most important development within e-journal systems (Caplan et al., 2001).

This paper describes the role of portal services and examines the current technologies associated with full-text linking. It will also briefly describe a portal service developed at the University of Illinois at Urbana-Champaign (UIUC) Grainger Engineering Library that features enhanced search and linking technologies. This service offers synchronous simultaneous searching of multiple information resources and provides full-text linking to locally licensed, available electronic journals. The Grainger service provides simultaneous searching of multiple periodical index databases, the online catalog, a Web search engine, several publisher full-text repositories, and local resources. The service's full-text linking capabilities utilize a local UIUC e-resource registry database, the CrossRef metadata database, and the article DOI.

SEARCH ACCESS THROUGH PORTALS

It is necessary for individual library systems to tailor their portals to reflect the institutional or consortial information resources licensed by and made available to their users. For example, access to the INSPEC database can be provided through local loading or via a number of vendors, including Ovid, SilverPlatter, or Axiom. In addition, the library or library system may be subscribing to remote publisher full-text systems, locally loading publisher full-text articles, and/or subscribing to full-text journals via a third-party aggregator, such as Ebsconet, Ovid, or OCLC Electronic Collections Online (ECO).

In particular, one of the primary goals of the library portal is to assist users and library staff in organizing and providing access to the growing number of publisher full-text journals. Indeed, electronic full-text journals have gained rapid acceptance by researchers and students (Saunders 1999, Hurd 2001). As Stackpole and King have noted, "the fundamental goal of the digital library . . . is to deliver the full content of library materials to the desktop" (Stackpole and King 1999).

There is also a widespread interest in providing the capability of user-managed or personalized information portals. This is exemplified by the MyLibrary project at North Carolina State University Library and other personalized library portal systems (Bonett 2001, Morgan 2000). These portal sites allow end-users to personalize the resources and, to some extent, the interface in order to reflect their individual user needs. The efficacy of this approach remains in question. At the present time, usage figures indicate that only a small core of users regularly access their MyLibrary type accounts (Ketchell 2000, Morgan 2000). These systems must be made extremely easy to set up or users will not take the time to use them (Nielsen 1998). More work remains to be done in this area.

Among the resources typically available to science and technology library users are: the local and consortial online catalogs (OPACs), locally loaded and remote periodical index databases that provide access to the journal literature, the rapidly growing number of discrete publisher full-text repositories, licensed aggregator sites that also include full-text resources, Web-based resources made available by researchers and companies, and specialized resources such as standards/specifications databases and patent databases. The local integration and linking of these resources requires a high level of customization and a great deal of ingenuity.

To address these issues, libraries and information providers have developed mechanisms to assist users with database selection, search strategy formulation, and search navigation (Ma and Cole 2001). One useful mechanism for addressing the problems of selecting from multiple relevant databases is to provide the capability of simultaneously searching multiple selected databases and returning individual search results for user examination.

PERIODICAL INDEX DATABASES

The availability of publicly accessible electronic periodical index databases has increased dramatically in the last ten years. For example, at the UIUC Library online article databases were first made available at public terminals in 1991. At that time, nine system-wide locally loaded periodical index databases and a number of library-specific CD-ROM databases were made accessible. In 2001, over 110 general and subject-specific Web-based periodical index databases are available campus-wide. Almost all the major A & I services now utilize a Web-based search engine.

Many of the A & I databases in the fields of science and engineering overlap in their subject focus and in their scope of coverage of the literature. Complicating this is the fact that almost all of the major A & I services in the Sci/Tech field perform selective indexing of the journals that they include in their coverage.

Deciding which of these databases best meets a specific patron information need is problematic for librarians, and is particularly difficult for patrons who are, increasingly, accessing these databases from offices, laboratories, and homes. The availability of customized subject-discipline specific gateway pages assists users in rapidly identifying relevant periodical index and other databases (Mischo and Schlembach 1999). However, there is some indication that users tend to most often select those databases that they have previously used (Meyer and Ruiz 1990), and it appears that many valuable specialized databases are underutilized (Hightower et al., 1998).

In fact, the overlapping Sci/Tech periodical index databases are a prime candidate for the application of simultaneous search algorithms.

SIMULTANEOUS DATABASE SEARCHING

As noted earlier, there are a number of vendor and library systems in various stages of production or development that provide simultaneous search and retrieval over multiple data resources.

One of the earliest multiple search vendor systems was the DialIndex system developed by the Dialog Corporation for their family of online databases, initially accessible over telnet connections. This system accepts user-entered search arguments expressed in Dialog command language and applies them to all the databases included in selected subject groups. DialIndex then returns the number of hits for each database. Any subsequent searching has to be done by re-entering the specific database. The primary value of this system lies in search strategy development. The Dialog Web version at <http://www.dialogselect.com/main.thtml> continues this technology of performing simultaneous searches over a set of databases.

Several of the OPAC vendors are committed to developing cross-content simultaneous search engines as part of their extended library system offerings. The MetaLib service from Ex Libris (see http://www.exlibris. co.il/metalib/) provides simultaneous search capability and the EnCompass (see http://www.endingosys.com/prods/encompass.htm) module of the Endeavor system will also provide this function. The Innovative Interfaces MetaFind (see http://www.ii.com/html/products/p_map.shtml) system is a universal search interface that allows access to multiple resources with a single search from a consistent interface.

In addition, the information providers are offering their versions of simultaneous search systems. Ovid is developing its Multifile and Deduping technologies, which operate over multiple A & I service databases (see http://www.ovid.com/documentation/features/v410/multifile. cfm). The Institute for Scientific Information (ISI) has announced the *ISI Web of Knowledge* system, which integrates journal, patent, and proceedings literature with Web resources and provides cross-resource searching. Likewise, the Gale Corporation has released the InfoTrac Total Access system which features simultaneous search capabilities over specified electronic resources (see http://www.galegroup.com/servlet/ ItemDetailServlet?region=9&imprint=000&titleCode=INFO26&type= 4&id=172049).

The search integration company Webfeat, with their Knowledge prism product, is marketing a sophisticated simultaneous database search system to libraries and corporations (see http://www.pksys.com/webfeat_ home.html).

On the library side, the University of California at San Diego developed a cross-database search system called the *Database Advisor* (Hightower et al., 1998). This system performed synchronous simultaneous searches over 25 science databases. The software and search technology developed in this project have been incorporated in the California Digital Library's *SearchLight* system (see http://searchlight.cdlib. org/cgi-bin/searchlight). *SearchLight* features simultaneous searching of databases in several subject areas under the general categories of science/engineering and social sciences/humanities. Also, the Los Alamos National Laboratory had developed the FlashPoint system as part of their Library Without Walls Project (Mahoney and DiGiacomo, 2001). FlashPoint provides a Web-based interface that performs a broadcast, parallel search of nine bibliographic databases.

There is a great deal of vendor interest in developing an overarching system architecture that will provide simultaneous search and discovery over multiple information resources. In particular, the integrated library system vendors are developing platforms that attempt seamless access services over a hybrid information environment, which includes publisher and vendor digital collections, specified Web resources, local collections of digital metadata, and secondary resources such as periodical index databases and the library online catalog.

FULL-TEXT JOURNALS

In addition to the growth of Web-enabled periodical index databases, there has also been an explosive growth in the number of electronic full-text journals. The Ulrichs International Journals directory lists over 25,000 online full-text journals as of August 2001. The UIUC Library presently provides access to over 4,700 full-text journals for its authorized users.

One commonly used tool that libraries are employing to simplify maintenance and to facilitate access to electronic journals is the e-resource registry database. This database contains metadata describing the electronic journal or other resource, including the target URL for the digital content, subject descriptor(s) for producing discipline-specific lists and Web pages, a persistent identification number, and other information such as publisher and ISSN. The custom subject lists can be generated both through librarian-specialist assignment and through user selection in the personalized environment. While this e-journal information can be incorporated into and served from the online catalog, it is often maintained in a separate Web-enabled database (Lakos and Gray 2000, Jordan 2000) or extracted from the online catalog and maintained in a separate database. See the Chan article in this volume for a detailed description of an e-resource registry. There is some evidence that users prefer a separate e-journal resource list rather than the online catalog when accessing full-text journals (Coonin 2001).

Full-text document representation standards are evolving. At the present time, most full-text links appear in extended citation displays in HTML format that include the article bibliography. The PDF versions of full-text articles are primarily used for on-screen viewing and printing. Web-based full-text employing HTML and XML markup languages will offer additional value-added functionality and will go beyond the present display of print journal surrogates (Mischo 2001).

LINKING TECHNOLOGIES

There are several important technologies that are playing key roles in linking between full-text article references within publisher repositories and portal implementations. These include the Digital Object Identifier (DOI) and its application in the CrossRef publisher initiative.

The DOI was developed by the Association of American Publishers and is now managed by the International DOI Foundation (IDF). It is both a unique and persistent identifier of a piece of digital content and a system to provide access to the content (Atkins et al., 2000). The DOI is an open standard for digital content identification. It is basically an alpha-numeric string that uniquely identifies a digital object. The DOI for a work remains the same forever, regardless of the publisher who maintains the intellectual property rights and the Web site to which the DOI resolves.

A DOI consists of the Registration Agency Prefix, the publisher prefix, and a publisher-assigned suffix or ID. An example DOI would be:

    10.1063/S0036915

where "10" is the Registration Agency Prefix, "1063" the publisher prefix, and S0036915 the suffix. The DOI suffix can be a dumb number or can be based on information such as journal name, volume, issue, and page.

The DOI and a URL that points to the digital object are then registered with the IDF. For example, the DOI 10.1063/S0036915 might be deposited with a target publisher URL of: http://www.pubsite.org/j1/apr99/art1.pdf.

The DOI and publisher URL are then loaded into the CNRI (Corporation for National Research Initiatives) Handle System Server, which generates a link URL such as: http://dx.doi.org/10.1063/S0036915 for identification and subsequent retrieval. It is this Handle Server URL that will serve as the link within an A & I Service entry or within an article bibliography link to the full-text article. The actual retrieval is done via a two-step process involving a redirection operation between the Handle Server and the user's browser. In this example, the URL http://dx.doi.org/10.1063/S0036915 is redirected to: http://www.pubsite.org/j1/apr99/art1.pdf.

The DOI standard is being utilized by the CrossRef consortium of publishers. The CrossRef members have established a collaborative reference linking service designed to create an environment where a researcher can click on a reference citation in a journal and immediately access the cited article (see: http://www.crossref.org/).

Publisher to publisher full-text linking has typically been done in the past via bilateral linking agreements involving publisher-specific protocols. The CrossRef consortium seeks to establish standardized linking practices. The CrossRef consortium was established in early 2000, with an initial membership of 12 STM publishers (Pentz, 2001). CrossRef is operated by the Publishers International Linking Association (PILA) and is presently comprised of 78 publishers from all disciplines, representing over 4,780 journals. The CrossRef publishers deposit DOIs for each journal article and also supply article metadata for a centrally maintained metadata database. The CrossRef consortium publishers have deposited over 3 million articles into the system.

In the CrossRef project, minimal-level metadata for each DOI is being deposited in a central database. This metadata database includes only the first author, the article title, and journal and citation information. There are no controlled vocabulary terms, abstracts, or additional authors.

One purpose of the CrossRef metadata database was to allow publishers to perform searches by author, journal title, ISSN, or citation (volume, issue, year) to extract DOIs in order to embed links into the bibliographies of their newly published articles. While this is not yet being done on a large-scale basis, the CrossRef metadata database allows other value-added providers (such as A & I services) and local link servers to query the database to extract metadata. The database also allows a "reverse metadata" lookup in which a DOI can be used to extract article-specific metadata.

It is important to note that the CrossRef DOIs do not typically link to a specific instance of a digital object, but rather will connect to a publisher presentation or "splash" page. This page may provide an extended citation of the specific article and will include the publisher's links to the various full-text instances, e.g., the PDF, HTML, or XML version(s).

GRAINGER SEARCH SYSTEM DESCRIPTION

As a working example of advanced search and linking portal technology, the Grainger Library at the UIUC has developed a Web-based module that provides simultaneous searching of the online catalog, the Compendex, INSPEC, Current Contents, and Applied Science and Technology databases, the Google search engine, and several publisher full-text repositories (Elsevier ScienceDirect, and the IEEE Institute of Electrical and Electronics Engineers full-text product).

Figure 1 shows the system's top-level interface in which users select the desired database services to search and enter search terms. This is a relatively simple interface that permits single term author, title, keyword, institution, journal name, and ISSN searches or Boolean AND or OR combination searches from multiple fields. In Figure 1, the user has entered the semiconductor material *AlGaas* (Aluminum Gallium Arsenide) in the keyword field to be combined with the author last name *Holonyak*. From here, the Search Aid software takes the user-entered search argument and normalizes it into the format expected by each of the database systems.

The searches are then performed synchronously and the numbers of search hits are displayed as they are returned. Figure 2 is a completed search results page indicating the number of search matches in each of the selected database services. The short entry results are displayed to the user, via a proxy server, from the actual vendor system that was searched. All subsequent links pass through the proxy server and are redirected to the vendor system with session connection information intact. The search results from the different database systems are not combined together in any fashion and duplicate citations from different services are not are eliminated. Rather, the user must view results from the desired single system. Multiple search service results must be viewed consecutively.

Figure 3 shows a user-selected short-entry search results display from the ISI Current Contents service. This database is accessed through an Ovid server. While the search results are displayed in the standard Ovid format, note that the proxy server has added links to the full-text of articles when those journals are available to UIUC patrons. The availability

FIGURE 1

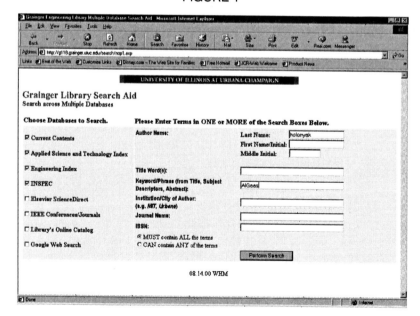

FIGURE 2

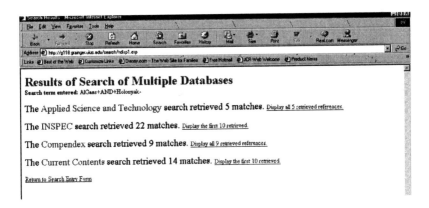

Results of Search of Multiple Databases
Search term entered: AlGaas+AND+Holonyak.

The Applied Science and Technology search retrieved 5 matches. Display all 5 retrieved references.

The INSPEC search retrieved 22 matches. Display the first 10 retrieved.

The Compendex search retrieved 9 matches. Display all 9 retrieved references.

The Current Contents search retrieved 14 matches. Display the first 10 retrieved.

Return to Search Entry Form

of a full-text version of a specific journal title is determined by an on-the-fly lookup in the UIUC custom e-resources registry database. When it is determined that the library has licensed full-text access to the specific title, selected metadata elements, including the first author last name, ISSN, journal title, volume, beginning page number, and year are extracted from the Ovid display. This information is then programmatically added to the full-text link in the value-added Ovid display shown here in Figure 3.

When the user clicks on the full-text link, the metadata elements contained in the link are used to perform a search in the CrossRef metadata database. From the returned CrossRef metadata results, the article DOI is extracted. The DOI is then resolved against the Handles Server to redirect the user to the specific article-level and full-text information at the publisher site. The full-text of the first retrieved citation is shown in Figure 4.

The metadata extracted from, in this case, the Ovid display is stored in the link and searched in the CrossRef database using the OpenURL protocol (Van de Sompel and Beit-Arie 2001). OpenURL (see: http://sfx1. exlibris-usa.com/openurl/openurl.html) is a standard for describing and transporting metadata between portal component sites. It is being utilized by local context-sensitive service components, also known as local link servers, that use the returned metadata from the citation to tailor a customized display for user action. The SFX server from Ex Libris is an example of a local link server.

FIGURE 3

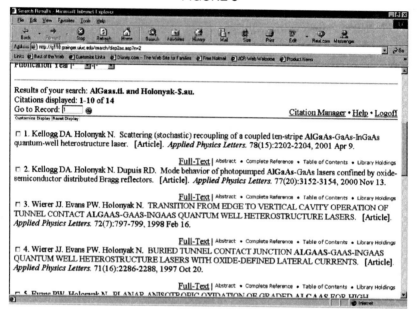

FIGURE 4

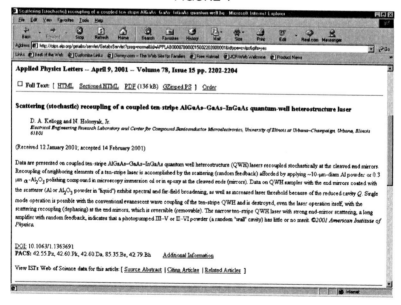

In a manner transparent to the user, the Grainger Search Aid utilizes simultaneous searching of periodical index databases, full-text availability displays determined from the UIUC e-resources database, and full-text resolution and display using a DOI obtained from the CrossRef metadata database.

Work is being done to add other additional periodical index databases and Web search engines into the Grainger simultaneous search system. It should be noted that the simultaneous search component and full-text article resolution function within the Grainger Search Aid could be applied separately within the software. It is expected that vendors and publishers will continue to incorporate and refine their searching and full-text linking functionality using many of the same techniques developed for the Grainger software.

CONCLUSION

As portal technologies evolve, libraries, vendors, and publishers will continue to offer enhanced search and linking mechanisms to provide custom user access to information resources. It is clear that integrated library system vendors and database vendors view simultaneous search and discovery as an important component in their umbrella system architectures. Simultaneous search services assist in the identification of appropriate information resources from among subject-related periodical index databases, online catalogs, and local and remote Web information resources available to the user.

In addition, the application of linking technologies such as the DOI and the widespread application of the CrossRef publisher initiative will result in ubiquitous linking between full-text articles and between periodical index databases and full-text resources.

The Grainger Library system described in this paper represents an attempt to incorporate and integrate simultaneous search and linking technologies, albeit within a limited domain. One of the key design challenges facing portal developers is the successful integration of search and linking within local and remote digital collections, local digital metadata, and traditional search tools such as periodical index databases and online catalogs. With the widespread adaptation of linking technologies, it is a propitious time to develop and refine these technologies. We can expect to see a variety of portal implementations designed to provide users with enhanced search and discovery and a one-stop-shopping approach to information resource retrieval and display.

REFERENCES

Atkins, Helen; Catherine Lyons; Howard Ratner et al. Reference Linking with DOIs. *D-Lib Magazine* 6, February 2000 (http://www.dlib.org/dlib/february00/02risher. html, accessed August 28, 2001).

Bonett, Monica. Personalization of Web Services: Opportunities and Challenges. *Ariadne* Issue 28, June 2001 (http://www.ariadne.ac.uk/issue28/personalization/, accessed August 28, 2001).

Campbell, Jerry D. "The Case for Creating a Scholars Portal to the Web: A White Paper" *ARL: A Bimonthly Report on Research Library Issues and Actions* 211, August 2000, p. 1-3 (http://www.arl.org/newsltr/211/portal.html, accessed August 15, 2001).

Caplan, Priscilla; Dale Flecker; Herber Van de Sompel; William H. Mischo; Edward Pentz; Larry Lannon; Timothy Ingoldsby. 2001. DOI Linking to the 'Appropriate Copy.' *D-Lib Magazine*, in press.

Coonin, Bryna "Digital Collections and TOCs vs. Full text" *Crossing the Divide: Coverage from ACRL's 10th National Conference, Part 2*, (http://www.ala.org/acrl/ denver01.html, accessed August 28, 2001).

Deiss, Kathryn J. "The Keystone Principles" *ARL: A Bimonthly Report on Research Library Issues and Actions* 207, December 1999, p. 8-9 (http://www.arl.org/newsltr/ 207/keystone.html, accessed August 15, 2001).

Guenther, Kim. 2000. "The Evolving Digital Library" *Computers in Libraries* 20 (February):48-50.

Hightower, Christy; Jennifer Reiswig; Susan S. Berteaux. 1998. Introducing Database Advisor: A New Service that will make your Research Easier. *College and Research Libraries News* 59(6):409-412.

Hurd, Julie M. "Digital Collections: Acceptance and Use in a Research Community" *Crossing the Divide: Proceedings of Tenth ACRL National Conference*, March 25-16, 2001, Denver, CO, p. 312-319 (http://www.ala.org/acrl/papers01/hurd.pdf, accessed August 28, 2001).

Jordan, William. 2000. My Gateway at the University of Washington Libraries. *Information Technology and Libraries* 19 (December):180-185.

Ketchell, Debra S. 2000. Too Many Channels: Making Sense out of Portals and Personalization. *Information Technology and Libraries* 19 (December):175-179.

Lakos, Amos and Chris Gray. 2000. Personalized Library Portals as an Organizational Culture Change Agent. *Information Technology and Libraries* 19 (December):169-174.

Liew, Chern Li.; Schubert Foo; K.R. Chennupati. 2000. A Study of Graduate Student End-Users' Use and Perception of Electronic Journals. *Online Information Review* 24(4):302-315.

Ma, Wei and Timothy W. Cole. 2000. Genesis of an Electronic Database Expert System. *Reference Services Review* 28(3):207-222.

Mahoney, Dan and Di Giacomo, Mariella. "FlashPoint@LANL.gov: A Simple Smart Search Interface" *Issues in Science and Technology Libraries,* Number 31, Summer 2001. (http://www.library.ucsb.edu/istl/01-summer/article2.html, accessed August 28, 2001).

Meyer, Daniel E. and Den Ruiz. 1990. End-User Selection of Databases–Part I: Science/Technology/Medicine. *Database* 13 (June):21-23.

Mischo, William H. and Mary C. Schlembach. 1999. Web-Based Access to Locally Developed Databases. *Library Computing* 19(1):51-58.

Mischo, William H. 2001. The Digital Engineering Library: Current Technologies and Challenges. *Science & Technology Libraries* 20(2/3):133-147.

Morgan, Eric Lease. 2000. Guest Editorial: The Challenges of User-Centered, Customizable Interfaces to Library Resources. *Information Technology and Libraries* 19 (December):166-168.

Nielsen, Jakob "Personalization Is Overrated" *Alertbox* October 1998 (http://www.useit.com/alertbox/981004.html, accessed August 16, 1991).

Pentz, Edward. 2001. CrossRef: The Missing Link. *College and Research Library News* 62 (February):206-209.

Stackpole, Laurie E. and King, Richard James. "Electronic Journals as a Component of the Digital Library" *Issues in Science and Technology Libraries*, Number 22, Spring 1999. (http://www.library.ucsb.edu/istl/99-spring/article1.html, accessed August 28, 2001).

Van de Sompel, Herbert and Oren Beit-Arie. "Open Linking in the Scholarly Information Environment using the OpenURL Framework" *D-Lib Magazine* 7, March 2001 (http://www.dlib.org/dlib/march01/vandesompel/03vandesompel.html, accessed August 28, 2001).

Zemon, Mickey. 2001.The Librarian's Role in Portal Development: Providing Unique Perspectives and Skills. *College and Research Libraries News* 62:710-712.

Index